50 STATES
500 SCARY PLACES TO VISIT

Publications International, Ltd.

Contributing Writer: Lisa Brooks

Images from Shutterstock.com, Wikimedia Commons

ISBN: 978-1-64558-736-1

Manufactured in China.

8 7 6 5 4 3 2 1

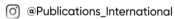

Let's get social!
@Publications_International
@PublicationsInternational
www.pilbooks.com

Contents

Alabama

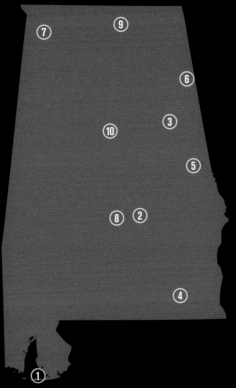

2. (Above) Huntingdon College (Montgomery)

If you visit Pratt Hall at Huntingdon College in Montgomery, Alabama, you might just encounter the ghost of a young lady named Martha. Better known today as the "Red Lady," Martha left her native New York and enrolled at Huntingdon in the early 1900s because it was her grandmother's alma mater. She was known on campus for her love of red: She decorated her room with red drapes and a red rug, and she often wore red dresses. Lonely and taunted by her peers, Martha died by suicide in despair. She now haunts Pratt Hall (which once housed her dorm), where residents occasionally catch a glimpse of a young lady dressed in red. In recent years, she seems to have gotten bolder, as students have reported cold blasts of air surrounding those who are caught picking on their classmates.

3. The Victoria Inn (Anniston)

Built in 1888 by Robert McKelroy for his family, the Victoria Inn served as a private residence before it was converted into a country inn in the mid-twentieth century. McKelroy built the house on the highest hill of Anniston's historic Quintard Avenue, and many say it is McKelroy himself who continues to stalk these halls and watch over the neighborhood from his mighty estate. Many of the ins's employees have reported hearing music playing from the music room when it was empty, glasses clinking in the kitchen, and absent footsteps walking all over the house.

4. Rawls Hotel (Enterprise)

Built in 1903 by Japeth Rawls, an innovative businessman who founded Coffee County's turpentine industry, the Rawls Hotel is said to be home to children who no longer play in this earthly realm. People have reported hearing children laugh on the third floor of the hotel as well as the kitchen when there were no children around. When restorations were underway in the late twentieth century, those who were working in the building reported seeing a young girl running down the hall. Many say Rawls himself also inhabits the building with these child-like specters.

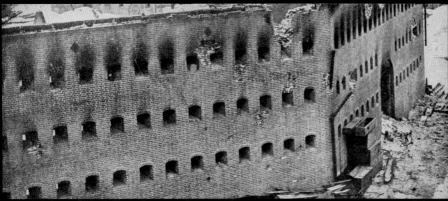

1. (Above) Fort Morgan (Mobile Point)

Fort Morgan has a long military history that perhaps contributes to the rumors of its haunting. Having operated during the Civil War, the Spanish-American War, and both World Wars, Fort Morgan has been the site of many battles and numerous gruesome scenes. Due to its long history, the site has been listed as a National Historic Landmark and is said to be one of the most endangered battle sites of the Civil War. Visitors have reported shadowy specters walking within the forts crumbling walls, mysterious sounds, and ominous feelings. These ghosts aren't the only vestige of battles of past eras: in 2007, a 90-pound live munition shell from the Union army was found on the site.

7. (Above) Belle Mont Mansion (Tuscumbia)

Built in 1832 by Alexander Mitchell, the Belle Mont Mansion was one of the largest plantations in antebellum Alabama with a large number of slaves who lived and worked on the grounds. The estate is said to be haunted by many of the plantation's former slaves. Some even say the the ghost of Mitchell resides here with them. The site was donated to the Alabama Historical Commission in 1983 and has undergone a total restoration. Today, it operates as a historic house museum.

5. (Above) Chambers County Courthouse (LaFayette)

Although no reports have been made of ghostly happenings inside of the courthouse—although it is the site of some uncouth history—many have reported a strange mist that surrounds the Joe Louis statue in the lawn of the courthouse. Joe Louis was a national hero who served in the Air Force during World War II and a famous heavyweight boxing champion from Chambers County, Alabama. His statue was erected in 2010 and the mist has been there ever since.

8. (Left) Old Cahaba (Cahaba)

The ghost town of Old Cahaba was once an important political site in Alabama as it once served as Alabama's first state capitol from 1820–1825. But due to flooding of the Alabama and Cahaba rivers, the city was abandoned in 1865. The ghost town is the site of three cemeteries—including a slave cemetery—and a Civil War POW camp. The Civil War POW camp, known as Castle Morgan, is said to be inhabited by many ghosts, including the ghost of Col. Christopher Claudius Pegues who was killed in battle in 1862. Since then, a glowing orb, first seen behind Pegue's home at the intersection of Pine and Chestnut streets, has roamed the abandoned streets of Alabama's lost capitol city and found refuge in the defunct POW camp.

6. (Above) Rock Run Mine (Rock Run)

The old furnace and commissary building at the abandoned Rock Run Mine is said to still be occupied by miners who were killed at the site when the mine was still in operation. The original building was built in the early nineteenth century, but during the Civil War, Union soldiers burned the building to the ground. The commissary was rebuilt in 1879, and was abandoned in the early twentieth century.

9. Maple Hill Cemetery (Huntsville)

10. Sloss Furnaces (Birmingham)

Alaska

2. Historic Anchorage Hotel (Anchorage)

Listed in the National Register of Historic Places, the Historic Anchorage Hotel is the only historic hotel in the Alaskan city. The Queen-Anne-style building, which was built in 1916, was considered one of the most elegant places in the city when it opened, hosting dignitaries and celebrities from Will Rogers to Herbert Hoover. But today, it has a reputation for hosting visitors of a supernatural kind. Guests have reported swaying curtains, pictures flying off walls, the sound of laughing children, and ghostly apparitions roaming the hotel hallways.

3. (Above) Begich Towers (Whittier)

To get to Whittier, Alaska, visitors must drive through a long, dark tunnel carved through a mountain. First impressions of the waterfront town can be unsettling, as blankets of fog often wend through the trees. While Whittier is popular with campers and hikers, full-time residents number fewer than 300. Most of them live in the infamous Begich Towers Condominium, where, they believe, they share their home with many ghosts. Whether whistling through the halls or stomping up and down the stairs, the noisy specters make life in the isolated town a little more interesting.

4. Russian Bishop's House (Sitka)

Built between 1841 and 1843, the Russian Bishop's House in Sitka, Alaska, is one of the oldest surviving examples of Russia's influence in the 49th state. Built as a home, office, and chapel for Russian Orthodox Reverend Ivan Veniaminov, it later served as an inn and a newspaper print shop. The house fell into disarray in the 1960s, but a 16-year restoration project returned it to its former glory. Tours are now available to the public, but be forewarned: visitors have reported being followed by the apparition of a woman in a blue dress.

1. (Above) The Alaskan Hotel (Juneau)

This spooky site—and oldest operating hotel in Alaska—is known for its haunted Room 315, an early twentieth century-era room from which a sailor once jumped out of and nearly died. This gold mining hotel opened in 1913 and continues to have a demonic influence over its guests.

5. (Above) Fourth Avenue Theatre (Anchorage)

A female ghost is known to haunt this 1940s Art Deco movie theater; the ghost's identity is unknown. It is also a respected architectural building that is listed in the National Register of Historic Places.

6. (Above) Kennecott Copper Mining Camp (Wrangell–St. Elias National Park and Preserve)

Alaska's frontier past has left it littered with abandoned settlements, train tracks, and mines. But perhaps none is so feared as the Kennecott Copper Mines, and the long-obsolete railroad tracks nearby. In its heyday, the railroad track helped haul 4 million tons of copper ore out of the mines; but the mining operation also cost untold lives. Even today, almost 80 years after the mine shut down, visitors to the area report seeing mysterious gravestones along the abandoned railway, which are later found to have vanished on a second look.

7. (Above) Red Onion Saloon (Skagway)

Thousands of prospectors frequented this 1890s bordello during the Klondike Gold Rush. Today, the saloon is a respected drinking hole. It's also the location of several ghosts, including "Diamond Lil," a madam during the Saloon's brothel days. Another spirit is "Lydia," a former prostitute who supposedly haunts the building's second floor.

8. Birch Hill Cemetery (Fairbanks)

Established in 1938, the Birch Hill Cemetery sits in a peaceful location in Fairbanks, Alaska, surrounded by dense woods. The cemetery overlooks City Lights Boulevard and the busy Steese Highway, where drivers catch a glimpse of the grounds as they drive by. Many passersby have reported seeing glowing lights dancing on the hill, but visitors to the cemetery insist they've seen even more. A specter named the "White Lady" is often seen at the site, as well as a little boy, both dressed in early 1900s garb.

9. The Diamond Center (Anchorage)

10. Golden North Hotel (Skagway)

Arizona

Map with numbered locations: 6, 1, 10, 8, 4, 7, 2, 5, 9, 3

2. Yuma Territorial Prison (Yuma)

Once named the "best haunted destination" in the country by readers of *USA Today*, the Yuma Territorial Prison in Arizona began housing criminals in 1876. It was only in operation for 33 years before closing due to overpopulation, but many believe that it is still occupied by the spirits of inmates today. Visitors report hearing angry voices in the empty hallways and seeing apparitions of death row inmates. But not all the ghosts are criminals—a little girl who drowned in the nearby Colorado River is said to sneak up on unsuspecting tourists and pinch them!

3. (Above) Bird Cage Theater (Tombstone)

The Bird Cage Theater in Tombstone, Arizona, is famous not so much for its performances, but for hosting the longest continuous poker game in history. Played around the clock from 1881 to 1889, the game was attended by the likes of Doc Holliday and Wyatt Earp. With such regular patrons, perhaps it's no surprise that 26 people were known to have died within the theater over the course of its operation, and many of them stuck around. Today, visitors report hearing phantom piano music, and see apparitions of everything from prostitutes to cowboys.

4. Hotel San Carlos (Phoenix)

Following its construction in 1928, the Hotel San Carlos was frequented by some of Hollywood's most famous actors, including Mae West, Clark Gable, and Marilyn Monore. It's also the site of a horrific tragedy that occurred shortly after its opening, when a 22-year-old woman jumped from the hotel's seventh story to her death. Today, guests report a pretty ghost that sits, cries, and haunts their rooms.

1. (Above) Hotel Monte Vista (Flagstaff)

Located just off historic Route 66 in downtown Flagstaff, Arizona, the Hotel Monte Vista has hosted numerous celebrities since its 1927 opening, including Bob Hope, Esther Williams, and Michael J. Fox. But the hotel is less renowned for its celebrity clientele than for its permanent, and ghostly, residents. Some of the most common sightings are of a woman in a rocking chair in room 305, and the figure of a bellboy who stands outside room 210. But most unsettling are the eerie cries of an infant coming from the basement, often heard by hotel staff.

5. Copper Queen Hotel (Bisbee)

The Copper Queen Hotel in Bisbee, Arizona, was opened in 1902 and boasts 48 Victorian-styled guest rooms. Every room in the hotel is different, giving them all distinct personalities. But the rooms aren't the only thing that gives this hotel personality; the site is also home to three ghosts. The first is an older, cigar-smoking man with a top hat and cape who resides on the fourth floor. The second is a woman named Julia Lowell, who died by suicide at the hotel. And the last is a small boy who mischievously moves guests' belongings.

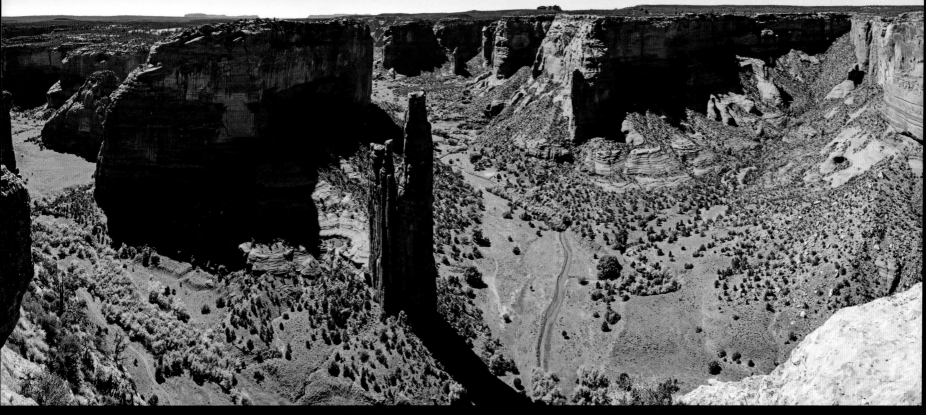

6. (Above) Canyon de Chelly

Located in northeastern Arizona, this national monument lies within the boundaries of the Navajo Nation. Despite its immense size of more than 80,000 acres, visitors report hearing distressing sounds that permeate throughout the area. Ghost hunters say those sounds are connected to an 1805 battle between the Navajo people and a Spanish military expedition that resulted in the deaths of more than 100 Navajo.

7. Casey Moore's Oyster House (Tempe)

You might not expect an establishment called Casey Moore's Oyster House to serve up anything but seafood, but this popular Tempe, Arizona, hangout is known for more than just fish. Built as a family home in 1910 by William and Mary Moeur, the house was purchased for use as a restaurant in the 1970s. Today, patrons believe that William and Mary continue to reside in the house, and neighbors have seen the glow of a light and the silhouette of a couple dancing in the upstairs window late at night.

8. The Vulture Gold Mine (Wickenburg)

9. Oliver House Bed and Breakfast (Bisbee)

10. (Above) Jerome Grand Hotel (Jerome)

Once the site of United Verde Hospital, the Jerome Grand Hotel opened in 1996 and continues to haunt its guests. Unexplained sounds, lights, and other paranormal activities afflict this creepy building where thousands of hospital patients reportedly died during the early twentieth century. A particularly haunted room is No. 32, where several suicides occurred.

Arkansas

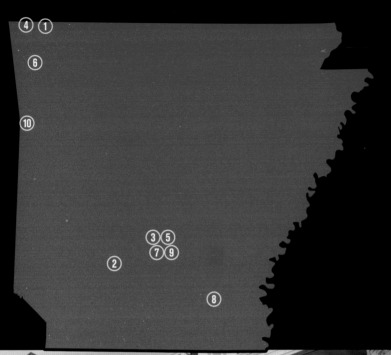

2. The Arlington Resort Hotel and Spa (Hot Springs)

With 500 rooms and suites, the Arlington Resort Hotel and Spa in downtown Hot Springs is the largest hotel in the state. Visitors to the famous mineral waters of Hot Springs National Park have frequented the hotel since 1875; Al Capone once stayed in Room 443. Today, guests in The Capone Suite, as it is now known, often smell cigar smoke in the non-smoking room. But the occurrences in Room 824 are even more unsettling, with visitors reporting flickering lights, items flying off shelves, and a bathroom faucet that turns on and off.

3. Mount Holly Cemetery (Little Rock)

Located in the heart of Little Rock, Arkansas, Mount Holly Cemetery is known for its park-like grounds and historic monuments. It is also the burial place of dozens of notable citizens of Arkansas, including former governors, senators, and literary figures. The cemetery is almost 200 years old, so it is not uncommon for visitors to report seeing the figures of Confederate soldiers or Native Americans roaming the gravesites. Some guests swear that the statues in the cemetery move, and that graves sometimes switch locations, making for a dizzying visit.

4. (Above) Pea Ridge National Military Park (Garfield)

In 1862, 23,000 soldiers fought in the Battle of Pea Ridge, one of the most pivotal battles of the Civil War. Thousands of men died to ensure the Union a victory and to secure Missouri for the United States. Today, this well-preserved battlefield is a national park with a theater, museum, and miles of hiking trails. With its violent past, it's no surprise that visitors to Pea Ridge often report an eerie feeling of being followed, as well as sounds of cannons and musket fire.

1. (Above) The Crescent Hotel and Spa (Eureka Springs)

The Crescent Hotel and Spa in Eureka Springs, was considered the most luxurious hotel in the country when it opened in 1886. But in 1937, a new owner, Norman Baker, converted the building into a hospital, promising a cure for cancer. Unfortunately, Baker was a charlatan, and many patients died after his experimental "cure." In the 1990s, the Crescent was restored to its former glory as a hotel, but according to many visitors, Baker's patients never left. They can often be glimpsed wandering the halls, and some even believe the hotel contains a "portal" to the world of the dead.

5. (Above) Arkansas State Capitol (Little Rock)

Built on the grounds of a former penitentiary, the Arkansas State Capitol is said to be haunted by a single ghost. This ghost may be the spirit of a former lawmaker, Ira Gurley, who was crushed to death in one of the building's elevators in 1932. But that's not the building's only spooky secret, some visitors today report creepy voices emanating from the capitol's basement.

6. Tilly Willy Bridge (Fayetteville)

The original Tilly Willy Bridge was demolished in 2010 to make way for a new bridge in 2012. The original bridge, built in the 1930s, was the site of a horrible accident when a car carrying a family plunged into a creek. Following the grisly wreck, passersby have reported seeing a ghostly apparition along the creek and a ghost car traveling along the old (and new) bridge.

7. Quapaw Quarter (Little Rock)

Much of the famous Quapaw Quarter neighborhood in Little Rock is haunted by numerous spirits.

8. The Allen House (Monticello)

Arkansas businessman Joe Lee Allen lived in this 1900s Queen Anne home until his death in 1917. In the late 1940s, Allen's daughter, Ladel Allen, died in the house after consuming cyanide. The room where the daughter died was sealed off for nearly 40 years. The house was later turned into apartments; the apartment tenants subsequently reported hearing unusual sounds and seeing shadowy figures.

9. MacArthur Park (Little Rock)

10. The Clayton House (Fort Smith)

California

2. (Above) Winchester Mystery House (San Jose)

At first glance, the Winchester Mystery House looks like a typical Queen Anne Victorian-style home. But inside the 24,000-square-foot mansion is a mysterious interior that many claim is haunted. Some of the doors and stairs to the 161-room home lead to nowhere, and spider web motifs and the No. 13 are used in various ways throughout the house. One thing is certain: this mysterious mansion is not to be messed with.

1. Queen Anne Hotel (San Francisco)

San Francisco is famous for its "painted ladies"—Victorian houses painted to enhance their architectural details—and the historic Queen Anne Hotel is decorated in such a style. Originally a girl's boarding school, the hotel is now haunted by Mary Lake, the school's headmistress. Her former office was housed in Room 410, and guests who have booked the room have reported encountering quite a friendly spirit. She has been known to unpack suitcases, sing guests to sleep, and even tuck them in!

3. (Above) Alcatraz Island (San Francisco Bay)

At times a military fort, a maximum-security prison, and the site of a months-long Native American protest, Alcatraz Island has a complex history. Now managed by the National Park Service, this island in San Francisco Bay is open to tours. As the former home to some of the most notorious criminals in history, including Al Capone and Arthur "Doc" Barker, it's no wonder that Alcatraz is considered one of the most haunted places in the nation. Voices, screams, sobs, and clanging doors are sometimes heard, and guests have even reported seeing an "entity" with glowing red eyes.

4. (Right) Whaley House (San Diego)

The Whaley House was the home of San Diego settler Thomas Whaley and his family. Whaley suffered some terrible personal tragedies in the home, including losing a toddler son to scarlet fever and a daughter to suicide. In 1960, the house opened to the public as a museum, and reports of strange activity began soon after. In addition to the sounds of a crying and giggling child, many have seen a young woman, appearing morose, gazing from an upstairs window after the museum has closed.

5. (Left) Castello di Amorosa (Calistoga)

In 1993, a vintner named Dario Sattui purchased 171 acres near Calistoga, California, and spent $40 million to create a castle to house a winery. Sattui's 141,000-square-foot winery, named Castello di Amorosa, is a faithful replica of a twelfth or thirteenth century castle, complete with a moat, drawbridge, a great hall, and even a torture chamber. While the castle itself is modern, rumor has it that some of the materials Sattui used to build it were old and possibly cursed. Staff say ghosts at the castle include a plague victim and a stable boy.

California

6. (Above) Hollywood Roosevelt Hotel (Los Angeles)

Opened in 1927 on the Hollywood Walk of Fame in Los Angeles, the Hollywood Roosevelt Hotel is the oldest continually operating hotel in the city. The hotel has hosted everyone from Marilyn Monroe to Brad Pitt, and it is also frequently featured in television shows and movies. But the same celebrities who patronized the hotel in life may also visit after death. It is said that Marilyn Monroe often appears in the mirror in room 1200, and other spirits in the hotel include Montgomery Clift, Carole Lombard, and a mysterious young girl.

7. Turnbull Canyon (Whittier)

9. (Above) Mission San Miguel (San Miguel)

This adobe building was the location of the terrible 1848 Reed murders, which claimed the lives of 11 people. More than 170 years later, the ghost of former owner Willaim Reed apparently haunts the old building. He's been seen wearing his navy peacoat as he roams around the church.

8. (Above) Battery Point Lighthouse (Crescent City)

Ghost hunters say three ghosts haunt the 160-year-old Battery Point Lighthouse. Caretakers report an empty moving rocking chair, footsteps moving along the lighthouse's stairway, and other paranormal happenings. The lighthouse remains open and available for public tours.

10. (Above) Suicide Bridge (Pasadena)

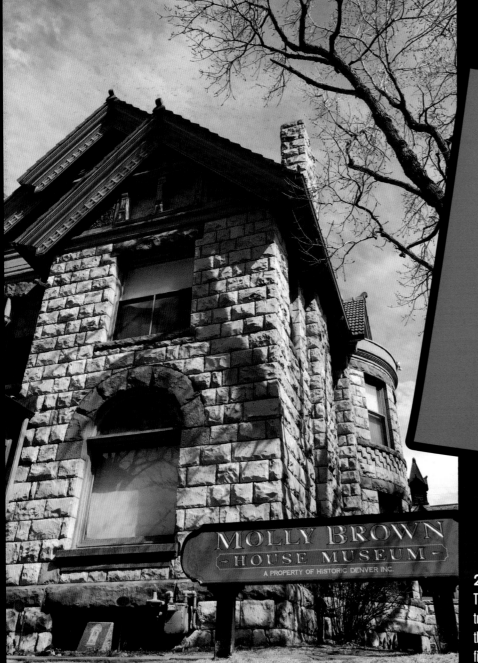

⑤

①②
④

③

2. Cheesman Park (Denver)

The spirits of the dead still haunt Denver's Cheesman Park. Locals blame an undertaker hired by the city to move the bodies prior to the park's construction. The undertaker, E.P. McGovern, haphazardly removed the bodies; some bones weren't even moved at all. No thanks to McGovern's sloppy work, mysterious figures, voices, and other creepy phenomena are seen and heard throughout this former graveyard.

3. Colorado Prison Museum (Cañon City)

Formerly a state women's prison, the Museum of Colorado Prisons in Canon City, Colorado, shares a wall with an active prison, the Colorado Territorial Correctional Facility. The women's prison dates back to 1935, and the museum opened in 1988. But according to visitors at the museum, the former inmates may still be around. The sound of voices, screams, and scraping furniture has been heard, and motion sensor lights have come on in empty, locked rooms. Occasionally, frustrated staff members mop up mysterious muddy footprints, only to have them reappear several days later.

1. (Above) Molly Brown House (Denver)

A survivor of the *Titanic* sinking, Margaret "Molly" Brown was a socialite and philanthropist who today is better known as "the Unsinkable Molly Brown." Brown and her husband acquired their wealth through mining operations near Denver, where they purchased a Victorian mansion in 1894. By 1970, the house was set to be demolished, but efforts to save it succeeded; the home is now open to the public as a museum. But some believe Molly never left. Visitors have seen flickering lights, felt cold spots, and seen the apparition of a woman in a Victorian dress.

No list of scary places would be complete without The Stanley Hotel in Estes Park, Colorado. The inspiration for Stephen King's classic, *The Shining*, the hotel was opened in 1909 as a health resort catering to sufferers of tuberculosis. By 1974, the hotel was a shadow of its former Victorian splendor, but the popularity of *The Shining* gave it new life. But King wasn't the first to find the hotel unsettling; ghostly activity, including shadowy figures, flickering lights, and phantom music, have been reported in every room of the hotel since at least 1940.

4. (Above) Brown Palace Hotel and Spa (Denver)

Built in 1892, the Brown Palace Hotel and Spa in downtown Denver, Colorado, is listed in the National Register of Historic Places. The hotel has hosted many U.S. presidents, the queen of Romania, and even The Beatles, but it is the ghostly visitors that get the most attention at this historic spot. Most commonly, guests encounter a spirit in a train conductor's uniform, who disappears into the wall if followed. Some have heard music coming from the empty ballroom. And, perhaps strangest of all, guests have seen something "scurrying" underneath the carpet in the lounge!

Colorado

6. Highlands Ranch Mansion (Highlands Ranch)
Erected in 1891, the massive Highlands Ranch Mansion is haunted by Julia Kristler, the daughter of Frank Kistler. Frank Kistler purchased the mansion in 1926, and his daughter supposedly haunts her bedroom; her cries are also heard throughout the home.

7. (Above) St. Elmo Ghost Town (St. Elmo)

St. Elmo was founded in 1880 as a mining town. For four decades, nearly 2,000 people called the town home, but in the early 1920s, the mining industry declined, and the population dwindled. Today, a handful of people still live in St. Elmo, but for the most part, the ghost town is an empty shell of its former self. And no ghost town would be complete without a ghost or two; St. Elmo's most famous spirit is Annabelle Stark, a former resident who is now often seen gazing from the upstairs window of a hotel.

8. Justina L. Ford Home (Denver)

This home of Colorado's first African American female doctor (also known as the Black American West Museum), the Justina L. Ford Home is haunted by a ghost who hovers among its rooms. The ghost is likely the spirit of Justina L. Ford; Ford lived in the home from 1912 until her death in 1952. The museum offers tours to the public each Halloween.

9. St. Cloud Hotel (Cañon City)

10. Henry Webber House (Aspen)

Connecticut

2. Curtis House Inn (Woodbury)

Former owners, guests, and employees are believed to haunt this eighteenth century inn's premises.

3. (Below) Norwich State Hospital (Preston and Norwich)

The Norwich State Hospital was in operation for more than 90 years when it closed its doors in 1996. Since abandoned, the hospital has become a popular site for vandals and curious explorers. Multiple deaths took place in the hospital during the early twentieth century, including two employees who died in a water heater explosion. But more sinister events also took place, including torturings and sexual assaults. Perhaps due to these unfortunate facts, the old building is a hotspot for paranormal activity.

1. (Above) Seaside Sanatorium (Waterford)

In the 1930s, it was common for those infected with tuberculosis to visit "sanatoriums" for treatment. Seaside Sanatorium in Waterford was the first such clinic specifically created to treat children. The building was later used as an elderly home and a hospital specializing in the treatment of mental disabilities. Closed and abandoned since 1996, the building now resides in a state park, but its dark history has left an imprint. Visitors have heard children's laughter and seen the abandoned playground equipment move of its own accord, lending an eerie atmosphere to this former hospital.

4. Gunntown Cemetery (Naugatuck)

Named after the Gunn family, one of the first European families to settle in Connecticut in the 1600s, Gunntown Cemetery was established in 1790. The cemetery, located in Naugatuck, is the final resting place of many Revolutionary War-era citizens who supported independence from the British. Famed paranormal investigators Ed and Lorraine Warren once insisted the cemetery is "officially haunted," and visitors agree. Many have heard children's laughter or music on the grounds, and some have seen a mysterious black dog, believed to be a harbinger of death.

5. Sterling Opera House (Derby)

The Sterling Opera House was the first building in the state to be listed in the National Register of Historic Places. Constructed in 1889, the opera house was also used as the town's city hall and police station. Now abandoned, the building has never been associated with stories of tragedy or death; but that doesn't stop the rumors of hauntings at the location. Some believe the building's namesake, Charles Sterling, continues to lurk in the shadows, while others claim to have seen the spirit of a little boy playing on the balcony.

6. (Above) Union Cemetery (Easton)

Considered by ghost hunters to be one of the country's most haunted cemeteries, Easton's Union Cemetery is home to a range of terrifying sights. Visitors have reported giggling children, men on horseback, cold spots, glowing orbs, and footsteps. The cemetery is also known for Red Eyes, a glowing pair of crimson eyes that spy on patrons, and the "White Lady," who appears floating in a white dress.

7. (Above) New London Ledge Lighthouse (New London)

A square, redbrick house topped with a circular lantern room, the New London Ledge Lighthouse in New London is one of the most unusual lighthouses in the country. The lighthouse was built in 1909 and manned by various crews of keepers until it was automated in 1987. But one keeper, a man by the name of Ernie who reportedly died by suicide at the lighthouse, never left. The last crew to man the lighthouse complained that the noisy ghost knocked on doors in the middle of the night, turned the television on and off, and pulled blankets from beds.

8. Bara-Hack Settlement (Pomfret)

The abandoned settlement of Bara-Hack in Pomfret has earned several nicknames, including "The Haunted Village of Lost Voices." This small enclave was founded in 1790 by Welsh settlers and named after the Welsh words for "breaking of bread." The community lasted less than a century however, and was completely abandoned by 1900, apart from those buried in the town's cemetery. After it was deserted, visitors to the area began telling tales of hearing voices and the sounds of horses and carriages, and seeing an apparition of an infant reclining in a tree.

9. Fairfield Hills State Hospital (Newtown)

10. Boothe Memorial Park (Stratford)

Delaware

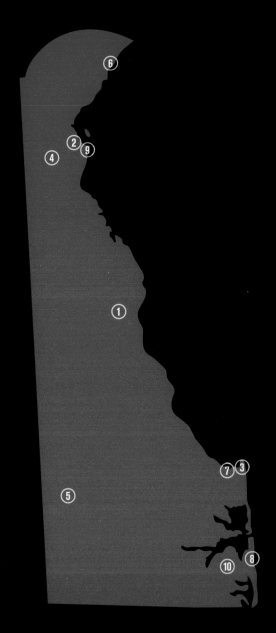

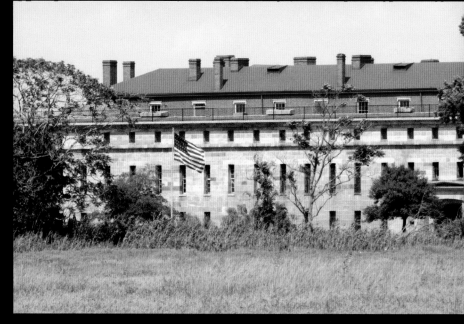

2. (Above) Fort Delaware (Delaware City)
This Civil War-era Confederate soldier prison camp is one of the county's most haunted places. Several thousand Confederates died at the camp, and their spirits supposedly haunt the site today. The fort features plenty of creepy tunnels where paranormal activity is ripe.

1. Governor's Mansion (Dover)
The Delaware Governor's Mansion in Dover is also known as "Woodburn." It was built in 1790 but was not used as an official governor's residence until 1966. With a history spanning more than 200 years, it is no wonder that many consider Woodburn to be the most haunted house in Delaware. The dining room is especially active, where residents have heard footsteps and seen figures in Revolutionary-era dress floating across the room. The ghosts also love to imbibe: one former governor would fill his wine decanter in the evening and find it empty every morning.

3. (Above) Cape Henlopen State Park (Sussex County)
Sitting on the Delaware Bay in Sussex County, Cape Henlopen State Park covers 5,193 acres. The beaches at Cape Henlopen were one of the first public lands in what would become the United States, set aside by William Penn himself. The area was also used as a strategic location during several wars, and concrete bunkers and fire towers dot the area. It is at one of these towers, fire tower 12, where visitors say they've encountered the spirit of a soldier, and some have seen his face in photos taken at the area.

4. (Above) Lums Pond State Park (Bear)

Lums Pond State Park spans 1,790 acres in Bear; it surrounds its namesake, the largest freshwater pond in the state. The park is a great place for activities like fishing, kayaking, and biking. Visitors can also hike the 6.4-mile Swamp Forest Trail—but they may have uninvited company along the way. According to legend, in the 1870s a girl was abducted and murdered along what is now the hiking trail. Her killer was never found, and some say the screams of her restless spirit can still be heard coming from the woods near the trail.

5. Old Maggie's Bridge (Seaford)

On an isolated, quiet stretch of road in Seaford, a crossing dubbed Old Maggie's Bridge borders a small stream. Legend has it that in the 1800s, a young, pregnant woman named Maggie Bloxom was traversing the bridge in a carriage when her horse got spooked and the carriage crashed into the water, decapitating poor Maggie. Today, ghost hunters say that Maggie wanders the area, looking for her lost baby. It is said that yelling, "Maggie, I have your baby!" will draw her to the bridge, where she sometimes appears, holding her head.

6. Bellevue Hall (Wilmington)

7. Cannonball House (Lewes)

As its name suggests, the Cannonball House in Lewes features a cannonball embedded into its side, a remnant of a battle with the British during the War of 1812. At one time, the house was used as the mayor's office, but today it is the home of the local Maritime Museum. Dating back to 1765, this historic spot is known for its fair share of ghostly tales, the most famous being the story of a girl named Sarah, who died in a fire. Now, visitors claim to hear footsteps and screams in the house, which are believed to be Sarah's.

8. The Addy Sea Inn (Bethany Beach)

This charming bed and breakfast is home to several ghosts. One of the Inn's bathtubs is known to shake for no discernible reason; in another room, organ music is often heard lulling guests to sleep. Nevertheless, the charming beachside establishment draws a steady stream of guests throughout the year.

9. Delaware City Hotel (Delaware City)

This once bustling nineteenth century tavern is today a seafood restaurant called Crabby Dick's. It's also a popular site for paranormal activity, like unusual noises and mysterious doors that randomly open and close.

Florida

1. (Above) Fort East Martello Museum (Key West)

Fort East Martello was built by the U.S. Army in 1862 to provide a defense for Key West during the Civil War. Today, it is managed by the Key West Art and Historical Society as a museum. But the biggest draw is not the collection of local art; rather, it is an allegedly cursed doll named Robert. Rumor has it, Robert can move, and even talk, on his own, and some say his facial features change. Tourists are cautioned to ask Robert's permission before snapping his photo, as bad luck has befallen those who don't.

2. The Cuban Club (Tampa)

El Circulo Cubano de Tampa, also known as the Cuban Club, is located in the historic Ybor City neighborhood of Tampa. Built in 1917 as a gathering place for Cuban immigrants, the building has had many uses, including a theater, bowling alley, spa, and library, among others. Today, the club is considered one of the most haunted places in Tampa and is home to several spirits, including an actor and a little boy. Photos taken in the building will often feature glowing orbs or ghostly faces.

3. (Right) Biltmore Hotel (Coral Gables)

When the Biltmore Hotel in Coral Gables was completed in 1926, it not only featured the largest pool in the world, but it was also the tallest building in Florida. Its 315-foot central tower was designed to resemble the Giralda, the bell tower of the Seville Cathedral in Spain. This record-breaking hotel is also believed to be home to many ghosts, especially on the thirteenth floor, where a mobster named Thomas "Fatty" Walsh was murdered in 1929. Some have also seen a woman in the tower, believed to have fallen to her death decades ago.

4. (Left) Key West Cemetery (Key West)

More than 100,000 people are buried on the grounds of this historic 19-acre cemetery. Patrons say the site is home to mysterious shadows, orbs, and voices. Visitors will also find humorous headstones, roaming chickens, and other oddities as they make their way around the cemetery.

5. Mary-Stringer House (Brooksville)

This creepy home, built in 1855, is today home to the Hernando Historical Museum. It was originally the site of a plantation, and dozens of slaves are believed to be buried on the site. Locals say the home is haunted by the spirits of two families that lived there before and after the Civil War.

Florida

6. (Left) St. Augustine Lighthouse (St. Augustine)

The St. Augustine Lighthouse was built between 1871 and 1874, and it is still a working lighthouse today. It is also a museum, where tourists can see the original nine-foot-tall Fresnel lens at the top of the 165-foot tower. More popular than the lens, however, are the alleged ghosts that roam the lighthouse. The most famous are Eliza and Mary, daughters of a lighthouse keeper who were killed in a tragic accident. Today, visitors hear their laughter and sometimes see small footprints on the floor of the lighthouse.

7. Castillo de San Marcos (St. Augustine)

This military fortification, constructed by the Spanish in 1672, later housed Native American prisoners and European soldiers. Today, a female apparition in a white dress, believed to be the wife of a former Spanish colonel, haunts the grounds. The ghosts of Spanish soldiers and the spirit of a Seminole have also been seen roaming the fortification.

8. Vinoy Renaissance Hotel (St. Petersburg)

The Vinoy Renaissance Hotel in is a Mediterranean Revival-style hotel, which was built in 1925. Throughout its history, the hotel has hosted celebrities ranging from actor Jimmy Stewart to baseball great Babe Ruth. In fact, major league baseball players often stay at the Vinoy, and many have had supernatural encounters. One player reported seeing the apparition of a man in his room, while another complained of water turning on and off repeatedly. Many guests have also complained of flickering lights, footsteps, and the sound of rattling chains.

9. Ashley's Restaurant (Rockledge)

10. (Above) Cassadaga Hotel (Cassadaga)

Georgia

1. (Above) Kehoe House (Savannah)

Built by William Kehoe in 1892, the Kehoe House in Savannah is one of the most photographed houses in the city. The inn was originally a home for Kehoe, his wife, and his 10 children, and later used as a boarding house and funeral parlor. Surprisingly, its history as a funeral parlor has not added to the house's spooky reputation. Rather, it is believed to be haunted by two of Kehoe's children, who are rumored to have died in the house. Guests hear children laughing and talking at all hours of the night, even when none are staying at the hotel!

2. (Left) Oakland Cemetery (Atlanta)

Considered by ghost hunters to be Georgia's most haunted place, Oakland Cemetery features a section where Confederate soldiers lie buried. Some have seen uniformed soldiers wandering the grounds and hanging from trees; others have spotted the spirit of Jasper Newton Smith, a powerful Atlanta businessman, rising from his grave and roaming the grounds.

3. (Right) Bonaventure Cemetery (Savannah)

Featured in the novel and film *Midnight in the Garden of Good and Evil*, Bonaventure Cemetery is located on the site of a former plantation. It became a public cemetery in 1907. The cemetery has its fair share of ghost stories, the most famous being that of a little girl named Gracie Watson. Some have said that Gracie's spirit appears to anyone who stands close to her grave, which is marked with a statue of her likeness. Others claim that Gracie's statue cries blood, and that other statues in the cemetery move and change expression.

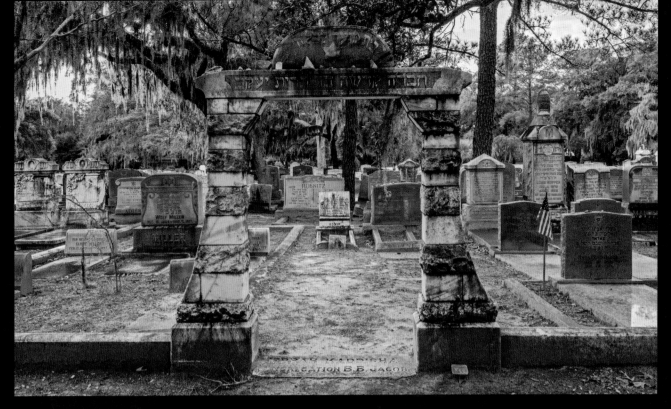

4. (Left) Hay House (Macon)

This 18000-square-foot Macon mansion is known for its spooky sounds, swaying chandeliers, and mysterious figures. It's also where a wedding photographer claims to have photographed a ghost in a top hat.

Georgia

5. (Above) Moon River Brewing Company (Savannah)
The Moon River Brewing Company is housed in the location of the first hotel in the city, which was built in 1821. The building was also used as a warehouse and an office supply store, and in 1876 it was used as a makeshift hospital to treat victims of a yellow fever outbreak. Perhaps for this reason, the building is now considered one of the most haunted places in America. Patrons report cold spots, flying liquor bottles, and ghostly apparitions. Many also hear the voices of children on the upper floors, where hundreds died from yellow fever.

6. (Left) The Marshall House Hotel (Savannah)
The Marshall House was built in 1851 and owned by a successful businesswoman named Mary Marshall. In 1864 the building was used temporarily as a hospital for Civil War soldiers, and it also housed patients during two yellow fever outbreaks. This history gives it a reputation for being one of the most haunted buildings in Savannah. Flickering lights, wiggling doorknobs, and faucets that turn on and off are often reported, as are the sounds of objects falling to the ground in the early morning hours.

7. (Left) Jekyll Island Club (Jekyll Island)

Once the secret meeting location for a group of the country's most powerful financial elite, the Jekyll island Club is also a hub for paranormal activity. The ghost of a man killed by a train in 1906 is said to haunt the premises, and a mysterious 1920s-era bellman is also known to make appearances.

8. Southeastern Railway Museum (Duluth)

Home to dozens of locomotives and railway cars, the Southeastern Railway Museum draws train aficionados to its 30-acre site in Duluth,. In addition to steam and diesel engines, freight cars, and cabooses, the grounds feature the original 1871 passenger train depot. According to some, they also feature restless spirits, including on the train that transported President Warren G. Harding's body back to Washington when he died in San Francisco in 1923. Staff have also seen shadowy figures in the museum after closing, and glowing orbs on the grounds.

9. Igbo Landing (St. Simons Island)

10. Windsor Hotel (Americus)

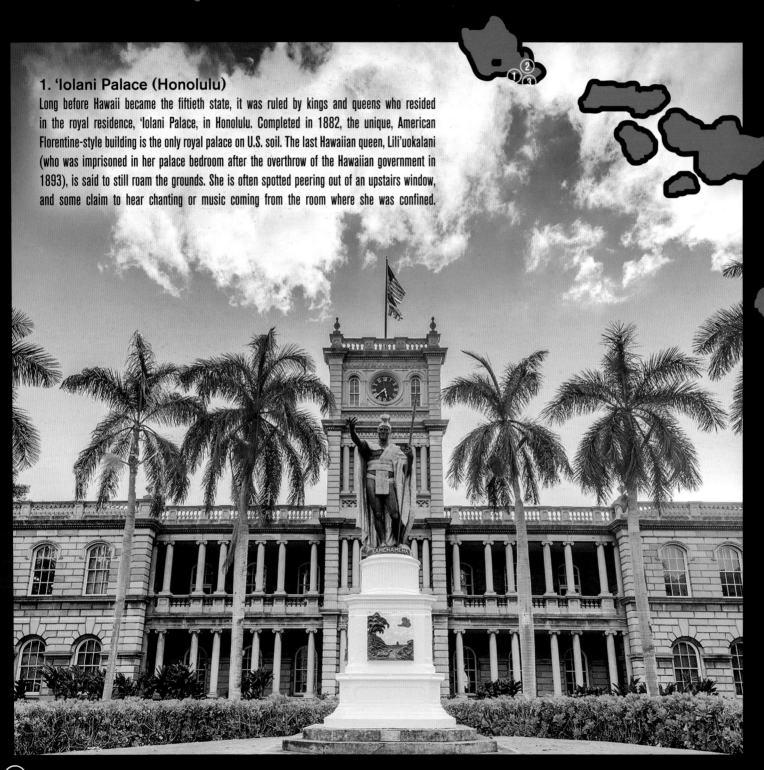

Hawaii

1. 'Iolani Palace (Honolulu)

Long before Hawaii became the fiftieth state, it was ruled by kings and queens who resided in the royal residence, 'Iolani Palace, in Honolulu. Completed in 1882, the unique, American Florentine-style building is the only royal palace on U.S. soil. The last Hawaiian queen, Lili'uokalani (who was imprisoned in her palace bedroom after the overthrow of the Hawaiian government in 1893), is said to still roam the grounds. She is often spotted peering out of an upstairs window, and some claim to hear chanting or music coming from the room where she was confined.

2. (Left) Nu'uanu Pali Lookout (Kaneohe)

Hawaii has no shortage of scenic locations, such as the Nu'uanu Pali Lookout on the island of Oahu. This cliff—"Pali" means cliff in Hawaiian—is located 1000 feet above the coastline and offers panoramic views of the Windward Coast of the island. While the spot is breathtaking during the day, at night the mood is a bit spookier. One story says that a girl died by suicide at the cliff after discovering her boyfriend was cheating on her. Now, if an unfaithful man stands on the cliff, she will call out his name, tempting him to jump.

3. (Right) Bishop Museum (Honolulu)

Also known as the Hawaii State Museum of Natural and Cultural History, the Bernice Pauahi Bishop Museum contains the world's largest collection of Polynesian artifacts. The museum was built in 1889 in honor of Bishop, who was the last legal heir of the royal Kamehameha Dynasty. Staff who work at the museum have reported seeing a shadowy figure wandering the building at night, and hearing crying. Many believe it is the ghost of a former worker who died after falling through the roof of the museum and hitting lava rocks below.

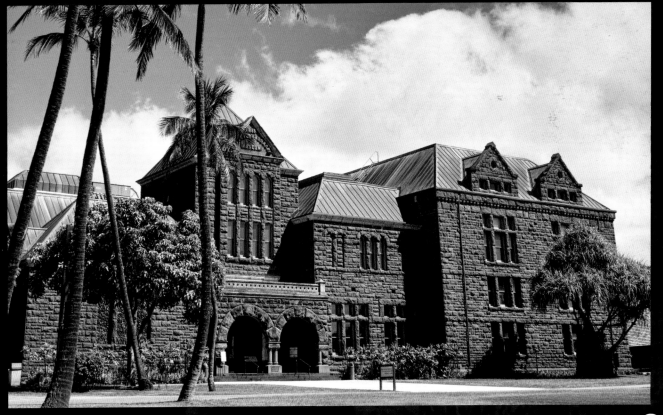

Hawaii

4. (Above) Pearl Harbor (O'ahu)
The ghosts of the men who died during the Pearl Harbor attack supposedly inhabit the Pacific Air Forces headquarters.

5. 16th Avenue Bridge (Honolulu)
The 16th Avenue Bridge in the Kaimuki neighborhood of Honolulu connects the two sides of the neighborhood that lie on either side of an interstate. The area is easily walkable, with sidewalks lining the residential street. Pedestrians walking over the bridge sometimes encounter an 8-year-old girl, who seems lost and asks for help. But as they cross the end of the bridge, the girl disappears. She is said to be the spirit of a girl who was killed on the bridge in a hit-and-run accident, now forever searching for her way home.

6. Kipapa Gulch (Mililani)
This creepy bridge, which was once the site of a significant battle, has been the site of multiple head-on collisions; voices and screams are supposedly audible from below the bridge. It's also where a mysterious band of "Night Marchers," or ancient warriors, are believed to roam the countryside. The "Marchers" apparently carry torches that illuminate the mountains.

7. Iao Theatre (Wailuku)

8. (Left) Hawaii Plantation Village (Waipahu)

Located in Waipahu on the island of Oahu, Hawaii's Plantation Village gives visitors a chance to see what life was like on an authentic sugar plantation. The 50-acre outdoor museum features many restored buildings and houses dating back to the 1800s. One of the most famous is the Portuguese House, where visitors often report seeing the ghost of a little girl who died in a fire when her father was working on the plantation. Abandoned by her mother as an infant, the girl now appears to women and children, searching for a mother and playmates.

9. (Right) Waipi'o Valley Lookout (Kukuihaele)

10. Thomas Hale Hamilton Library (Honolulu)

Hawaii's largest research library is home to unusual voices, apparitions, and a woman dressed in pink who roams the library's first floor. The spirit of a student who died by suicide in the 1990s apparently haunts the library's ninth floor.

Idaho

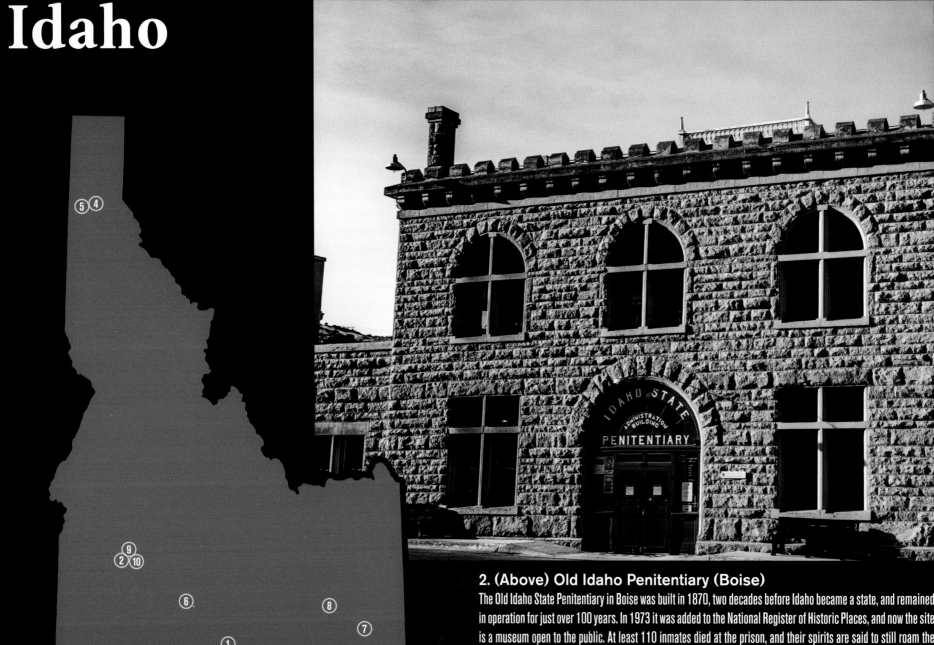

1. Stricker Ranch (Hansen)

Once a part of the Oregon Trail, the Sticker Ranch was a popular stagecoach stop in the late nineteenth century. A house was built on the property in 1901 by Herman Stricker; Stricker's wife, Lucy Walgamott, cared for sick emigrants who stayed at the ranch, including those who died. Locals say the spirits of the departed regularly haunt the property.

2. (Above) Old Idaho Penitentiary (Boise)

The Old Idaho State Penitentiary in Boise was built in 1870, two decades before Idaho became a state, and remained in operation for just over 100 years. In 1973 it was added to the National Register of Historic Places, and now the site is a museum open to the public. At least 110 inmates died at the prison, and their spirits are said to still roam the grounds. Visitors claim to hear strange sounds and voices, especially near the cell once used for solitary confinement.

3. Howell's Opera House (Oakley)

When it was built in 1907, Howell's Opera House was one of the only theaters between Salt Lake City and Boise. The building was almost demolished in the 1970s, but local residents raised funds to save and restore the theater. Today, according to staff and many theatergoers, the opera house is home to the ghost of a dark-haired woman who is often seen backstage. She has even been spotted on stage during performances, blending in with crowds of actors. No one knows who she is, but she seems to enjoy the limelight.

4. The Brig at Farragut State Park (Athol)

Formerly the site of a U.S. Navy training station, Farragut State Park near Athol is a popular spot for recreational activities like camping and hiking. Of the hundreds of buildings once used for the training station, few remain. But the still-standing former confinement facility now houses the Museum at the Brig, which features naval and war memorabilia. Many visitors also believe the former jail is home to a ghost, who appears as an apparition wearing a military uniform. Employees and guests have both seen the spirit and reported objects moving within the jail cells.

7. Enders Hotel and Museum (Soda Springs)

Initially a commercial establishment, Enders Hotel formally opened as a hotel in the 1930s. It was a popular spot for social events, including weddings, balls, and other receptions. Today, the building's second story is supposedly haunted by strange spirits known to rearrange objects and strike chills in the backs of the hotel's guests.

5. (Above) Spirit Lake (Kootenai County)

Spirit Lake is a tiny town in Kootenai County that borders a lake of the same name. According to the locals, the lake was named after a tragic event long ago. Legend says that the chief of the Kootenai Tribe had promised his daughter in marriage to a warring tribe, in order to secure peace. However, his daughter loved another man, and together, the couple ran away to the lake, where they jumped to their deaths. Now, many say that on still nights, the spirits of the couple can be seen drifting across Spirit Lake in a canoe.

6. Shoshone Ice Caves (Shoshone)

Lava and ice don't normally go together, but the Shoshone Ice Caves would not have formed without the help of volcanic activity. Today, these ancient lava tubes, 100 feet below the surface of the rocky ground, remain at a chilly 30 degrees year-round, freezing subterranean water. Legend says that a Native American princess was buried in the caves; the princess now wanders the tunnels searching for an escape from her icy grave. Guides have reported hearing footsteps and voices in the caverns when all the tourists have gone.

8. (Above) Pocatello High School (Pocatello)

A security camera at the high school in 2014 captured a shadowy figure walking in and out of a bathroom. Some believe that the figure is the spirit of a girl who died by sucide in the school decades earlier. Several other deaths have occurred on the school's grounds over the last 100 years.

9. Idanha Building (Boise)

10. The Owyhee (Boise)

Illinois

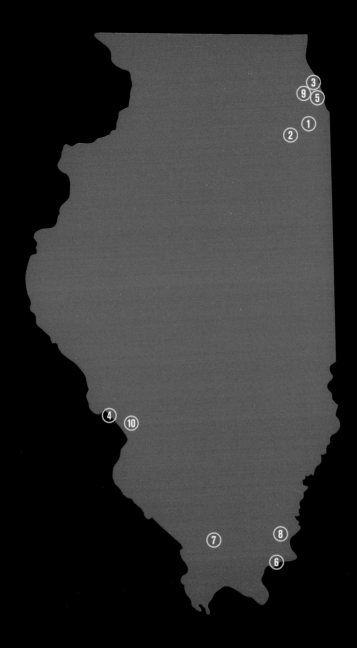

2. (Above) Old Joliet Prison (Joliet)

The castle-like Old Joliet Prison in Illinois was built in 1858 and was in operation until 2002. It may be best known for its appearances in movies and television, including the 1980 film *The Blues Brothers* and the Fox Network show *Prison Break*. Since 2018, the prison has offered tours of the grounds, including a popular "haunted history tour." With a violent past of riots, suicides, and murders, it's no wonder that many believe tormented spirits haunt the site. Visitors often report feeling malevolent energy and hearing angry voices.

1. Bachelor's Grove Cemetery (Midolthian)

Located in the southwest Chicago suburb of Midlothian, Bachelor's Grove Cemetery contains 200 graves that date back to 1834. The small graveyard was abandoned by the turn of the century, and eventually the overgrown, unkempt site became a hangout for teenagers and vandals. Today, the cemetery is best known for its many ghost sightings, including apparitions of a lady in white, men dressed in monk's robes, a farmer and his horse, and a black dog. Many also see floating orbs of light and vehicles that appear and disappear.

3. (Above) Lincoln Park Zoo (Chicago)

Chicago's famous and sprawling zoo was constructed over a former cemetery. Hundreds or even thousands of corpses may remain buried on the these grounds, which could be why park patrons have reported seeing ghosts in Victorian-era clothing walking throughout this popular city zoo.

4. McPike Mansion (Alton)

Paranormal activity floods this nineteenth century mansion. Apparitions, child laughter, and other sinister events are common during haunted house tours. Locals say the home is haunted by the spirits of a former owner and servant.

7. Hundley House (Carbondale)

On the evening of December 12, 1928, banker J.C. Hundley and his wife, Luella, were shot to death in their house in Carbondale. Although Hundley's son was suspected in the killings, he was acquitted and the murders were never solved. Subsequent owners of the house throughout the years have often reported ghostly activity within its walls, including slamming doors and televisions turning on and off. Even passersby find the house creepy, with some seeing the porch swing moving on its own or hearing gunshots coming from the house.

5. (Above) Hull House (Chicago)

Originally owned by Charles Jerald Hull, Hull House was a Chicago settlement house founded in 1889 by Jane Addams and Ellen Gates Starr. Now a museum, Hull House is perhaps most famous for the legend of the "Devil Baby," a deformed baby who was left on the doorstep of the house. Residents took in the infant, which was believed to be cursed, and hid it within the house, where it still appears to visitors today. Addams always denied that the baby existed; but she did claim to know of another famous ghost, the Lady in White, who appears in bedrooms on the second floor.

6. Rose Hotel (Elizabethtown)

The Rose Hotel, located on the banks of the Ohio River, is one of the oldest structures in Illinois; it was originally built in 1812. During renovations on the property in the early 2000s, the remains of several unknown persons were discovered on the grounds but were left untouched. Many believe that these people, whoever they were, continue to make the hotel their home. Guests report seeing mist, glowing orbs, spirits in the hallways, and ghostly faces in pictures taken on the property.

8. (Above) Crenshaw House (Junction)

This 1830s-era home, built by slave trader John Hart Crenshaw, was part of the Reverse Underground Railroad; the house was a spot where free blacks were illegally held before being sold into slavery. Also known as "The Old Slave House," the home is supposedly haunted by the spirits of the captured free blacks.

9. H.H. Holmes' Murder Castle (Chicago)

10. Lincoln Theatre (Belleville)

Indiana

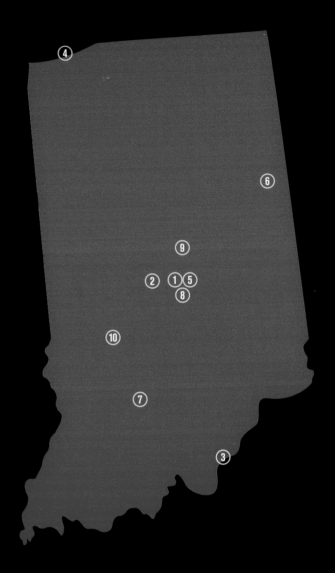

2. (Above) The Haunted Bridge (Avon)

The seal of the town of Avon features a local railroad bridge. Constructed in the 1850s, the bridge has a reputation for being one of the most haunted locations in the state. One legend says that when the bridge was being built, a worker fell into a cement pylon. Unable to extract his body, his coworkers nonetheless used the pylon in the bridge construction. For decades afterwards, passersby swore they heard screams and knocking coming from inside the structure. Today, many insist that a ghostly apparition wanders the tracks, attempting to flag down a train.

3. (Above) Culbertson Mansion (New Albany)

Culbertson Mansion, built in 1867, was home to businessman William Culbertson, who was once the richest man in Indiana. Located in New Albany, the 20,000-square-foot home is now a state historic site open for tours. The house is often used as a "haunted house" attraction during the Halloween season, but many believe the ghosts in this mansion are real. Staff have reported lights turning off and on, smelling cigar smoke in empty rooms, and seeing the apparition of a maid who is believed to have died in the house.

1. Nicholson-Rand House (Indianapolis)

An example of the American version of Gothic Revival architecture popular in the mid-nineteenth century, the Nicholson-Rand House in Indianapolis was built by David Nicholson in 1876 and later became the home of John Lindsay Rand and his family. In 1997, the house was moved half a mile to a new location to save it from demolition, and a newspaper photographer took a picture of the empty house for a story. When it was published, many were chilled to see what looks like the image of a ghost in an upstairs bedroom.

4. (Right) Diana of the Dunes (Indiana Dunes National Park)

Alice Mabel Gray was born in Chicago in 1881. Intelligent and educated, Gray became disillusioned with her life in the city and in 1915 she moved to a shack in the sand dunes along Lake Michigan in northwestern Indiana. A free spirit who enjoyed solitude, Gray soon earned the nickname "Diana of the Dunes" from the locals, who often saw her along the beach. After she died of kidney failure in 1925, reports of a ghostly figure wandering the dunes began to circulate. Many believe Gray continues to walk the beach in solitude.

5. Hannah House (Indianapolis)

Located on Indianapolis' south side, this creepy 24-room house was once a popular hiding spot for runaway slaves. On one fateful evening, a flipped over oil lamp caused a massive fire in the home's basement, killing numerous slaves. The spirits of those departed victims are said to haunt the home today.

6. Finch Cemetery (Portland)

Some of the saddest sights in any cemetery are the graves of children. At Portland's Finch Cemetery, one child's grave reportedly lends a strange energy to the location. Named Cinderella Steed, the child was born in 1858 and died only a year and a half later in 1859. Legend has it that the number of gravestones on the way to Cinderella's plot add up to 13; but on the way back, only 11 gravestones are visible.

7. French Lick Springs Hotel (French Lick)

8. James Allison Mansion (Indianapolis)

This creepy Arts & Crafts-style mansion is thought to be haunted by the spirit of a small girl. The girl, legend says, drowned in the home's basement pool. Voices, mysteriously moving objects, and the girl's apparition are all frequent occurrences on these haunted grounds.

9. Roads Hotel (Atlanta)

This 1890s-era property was once purchased by Newton Roads; many of his family members later died on its grounds. Throughout the early twentieth century, the site was a popular spot for criminals like Al Capone and John Dillinger. In recent years, a variety of apparitions have been reported, including those of children, men, and women. Unusual sounds and voices are also commonplace.

10. Zion United Church of Christ Cemetery (Poland)

Iowa

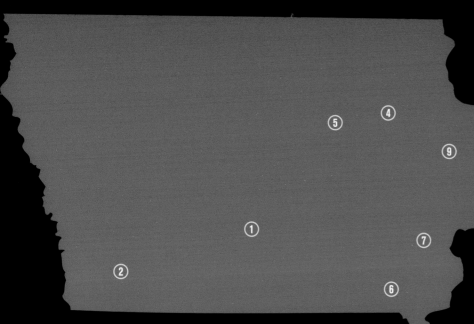

2. Villisca Ax Murder House (Villisca)

It's not hard to guess what happened in the Villisca Axe Murder House in Villisca on June 9, 1912. But the brutal murders of Josiah and Sara Moore, their four children, and two houseguests have remained unsolved for more than a hundred years. With such a horrifying past, it's unsurprising that all kinds of ghostly activity have been reported at the house. Footsteps, voices, apparitions, and glowing orbs are common. Many visitors bring toys for the Moore children, which are said to move on their own as the spirits play.

1. (Above) Jordan House (West Des Moines)

The Jordan House in West Des Moines was built by abolitionist James C. Jordan in the 1850s and used as a station on the Underground Railroad. Famous abolitionist John Brown stayed at the Jordan House at least twice, using the home as a stopover before leading freed slaves to Canada. But the house was also the site of tragedy; it's where Jordan's three-year-old daughter, Eda, died in an accident. Today, visitors to the historic building often hear a child singing and talking, and some have even seen Eda's ghost playing in different rooms of the house.

3. (Above) Ambrose Hall (Davenport)

St. Ambrose University's Ambrose Hall is home to a myriad of unsettling occurrences, including odd noises, footsteps, and flickering lights. The spirit of a former priest may be the culprit. In addition to its general creepiness, the late nineteenth century-era building is listed in the National Register of Historic Places.

7. Lover's Leap Swinging Bridge (Columbus Junction)

Located eight stories above a ravine in Columbus Junction, the Lover's Leap Swinging Bridge dates back to the 1800s. According to legend, an Indian maiden, heartbroken after her lover was killed in a battle, threw herself into the ravine. It is said that the forlorn maiden is still buried in the earth under the bridge, and those who cross the bridge at night can hear the echoes of her mournful cries. After a 1920 incident in which two boys fell from the bridge but survived unscathed, many believe the ghost is a protector.

8. Mathias Ham House (Dubuque)

The Mathias Ham House was named for the Dubuque businessman who owned it. Built in the mid-1800s, the home has been restored and is listed in the National Register of Historic Places. Many members of the Ham family lived and died in the house, including Mathias himself. Ham's daughter, Sara, who lived alone in the house after her parents died, shot and killed an intruder who entered the home one night. Vsitors say that Ham and the intruder both haunt the home, with many reporting cold spots, flickering lights, footsteps, and phantom organ music.

9. Edinburgh Manor (Monticello)

4. (Above) Independence State Hospital (Independence)

This former psychiatric hospital is a paranormal hotspot. It once housed the criminally insane, mentally ill, and other addicts; it was also where doctors performed disturbing procedures on their patients like electric shop therapy and lobotomies. Visitors today report unusual voices, screaming, and cold drafts.

5. Eldora Rotary Haunted Hospital (Eldora)

With a population of less than 3,000, the town of Eldora is best known for being a filming location for the 1996 movie *Twister*. But around Halloween, the town is also known for hosting what many think is the best haunted house attraction in Iowa, the Eldora Rotary Haunted Hospital. Located in an abandoned wing of a former hospital, the haunted house provides plenty of scares while also raising money for Eldora. But with its history of housing the sick and dying, perhaps this creepy abandoned building houses spirits, too.

6. Mason House Inn (Bentonsport)

Initially a resting spot for steamboat travelers and later a hospital, the Mason House Inn is supposedly haunted by a man named Knapp. Knapp, locals say, was murdered in the Inn, and his presence never left. Other oddities, such as footsteps and a floating Victorian dress, have also been reported by the Inn's guests.

10. (Above) Hotel Blackhawk (Davenport)

Kansas

1. (Right) Brown Grand Theatre (Concordia)

Built by Napoleon Bonaparte Brown and his son, Earl Van Dom Brown, the Brown Grand Theater in Concordia was a sight to behold when it opened in 1907. The Renaissance-style building was declared "the most elegant theater between Kansas City and Denver." In 1980, during a restoration project, workers reported seeing a figure dressed in period clothing in the balcony. Since then, others have seen a shadowy apparition moving in different areas of the theater. Many are convinced it is the ghost of Earl, who loved the theater so much he now refuses to leave.

Spanning a creek near Valley Center, Theorosa's Bridge has been the source of eerie legends for decades. Although several versions of the legend exist, the story always features a mother losing a child. Sometimes the mother's name is Theorosa, and her baby has been stolen or thrown into the creek; other times, the baby's name is Theorosa, and the mother wanders the creek, calling her name. Drivers crossing the bridge often insist they hear sobbing or a crying baby, and some have seen the ghostly figure of a woman on the bridge.

7. Molly's Hollow (Atchison)

Considered by some to be the most haunted town in Kansas, Atchison is the home of Jackson Park, a 100-acre property with views of the Missouri River. But the park is also known for the tragic story of Molly's Hollow. According to legend, Molly was an African American girl who was attacked by a racist mob and hung from a tree in the park. Visitors to the hollow report hearing screams coming from the area after dark, and some have even claimed to see Molly's apparition hanging from a tree.

8. (Above) Old Cowtown Museum (Wichita)

Old Cowtown Museum sits on land just off the original Chisholm Trail. The open-air history museum was established in 1952, and it features dozens of buildings that date back to the 1800s. One of the older buildings in the museum was the home of newspaper editor Marshall Murdock; it is also said to be the most haunted area on the site. Visitors have heard windchimes and footsteps and seen the ghost of Murdock's daughter playing in the house.

9. St. Jacob's Well (Ashland)

10. Brown Mansion (Coffeyville)

2. (Above) Fort Leavenworth (Leavenworth)

This active military installment is one of the oldest United States Army posts. Situated on a sprawling tract of land, the installment is haunted by former soldiers, a murdered priest, and a woman who lost her children.

3. Eldridge Hotel (Lawrence)

The ghost of Civil War Colonel Shalor Eldridge supposedly haunts Room 506. Locals say he's friendly, however, and generally means no harm. The hotel was added to the National Register of Historic Places in 1986.

4. Stull Cemetery (Stull)

Stull is a "blink and you'll miss it" tiny town, located about halfway between Topeka and Lawrence. It would probably be forgettable were it not for an urban legend that insists the Stull Cemetery is the evilest place on earth. In fact, according to some, the cemetery contains a literal "gateway to hell." The story was highlighted in a 1974 issue of *The University Daily Kansan*, and since then, many have told stories of strange occurrences inside the cemetery. Some even believe the residents of Stull may be witches themselves!

5. Sallie House (Atchison)

This ordinary-looking home packs a spooky punch. Built in the late nineteenth century, legend says a young girl named Sallie died at the home during a surgery to remove her appendix. Ghost hunters say Sallie's spirit still roams the house today. Visitors to the home have reported a variety of spooky occurrences, such as moving objects, unusual scratches and bruising, and mysterious coldness.

Kentucky

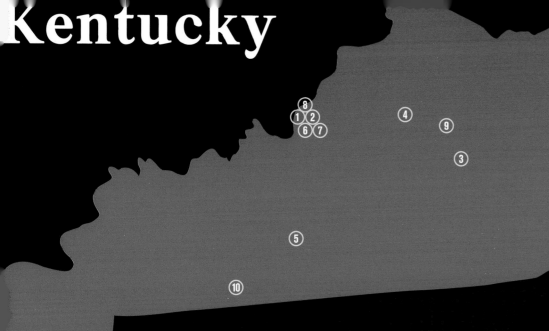

E.P. Tom Sawyer State Park in Louisville is situated on land that was former~~~ occupied by Kentucky's Central State Hospital, also known as Lakelan~ Asylum. Although the building was demolished in 1996, an undergroun~ cave that was used for cold storage, now known as Sauerkraut Cave~ is still located in the park. The asylum was reportedly a place ~ torture and neglect, with many patients dying in the hospita~ Those who venture into the cave say they can hear ghost~ music and voices and feel phantom tugs on their clothing~

3. White Hall State Historic Site (Richmond)

This intimidating 44-room Italianate mansion was built by Kentuck~ legislator Cassius Marcellus Clay in the late 1790s. Locals claim th~ home is haunted by Clay, his wife, and his son. Guests have observed suc~ paranormal oddities as moving candles, footsteps, and random noises at the historic hom~

1. (Above) Waverly Hills Sanatorium (Louisville)

Originally used to house tuberculosis victims, Louisville's Waverly Hills Sanatorium was opened in 1910, but it closed down in 1961 thanks to antibiotic advancements that made the illness treatable. Sadly, it is estimated that approximately 6,000 people died within the sanatorium. Its history of sickness and death has given it a reputation for being one of the most haunted hospitals in the U.S. Visitors have seen shadowy figures lurking

4. (Above) Liberty Hall (Frankfort)

Kentucky founding father John Brown started construction on his family's Frankfort home in the

5. Mammoth Cave (Mammoth Cave National Park)

This cave system, thought to be more than 4,000 years old, is downright creepy. Parts of the complex were used as a healing site for nineteenth century tuberculous patients. The spirits of the deceased haunt the cave today.

6. Mitchell Hill Road (Fairdale)

In the mid-twentieth century, thrill-seeking teenagers used to race their cars up and down a stretch of road in Fairdale nicknamed "Hot Rod Haven." Today, it's known as Mitchell Hill Road; according to legend, it was the site of a terrible accident in the 1940s. According to the story, a girl died when she and her boyfriend crashed their car at the bottom of a hill on their way to the prom. Now, people who drive along this stretch of Mitchell Hill often report seeing a girl in a prom dress wandering along the road.

8. Sleepy Hollow Road (Louisville)

In the daytime, a drive down Sleepy Hollow Road near Louisville can be quite pleasant. The winding country road is bordered by high treesss which canopy the road in greenery. But at night, that same canopy feels menacing, and the trees block out even the brightest moonlight. Legend says that a phantom hearse roams the eerie location at night, following unsuspecting cars and sometimes running them off the road. Some say that time is lost on Sleepy Hollow, too; a drive that seemed only a few minutes will turn out to have been hours.

9. Loudon House (Lexington)

10. Octagon Hall Museum (Franklin)

7. (Above and Right) Eastern Cemetery (Louisville)

Eastern Cemetery in Louisville is an abandoned 28-acre cemetery that dates back to 1844. Although there are only 16,000 graves at the site, more than 130,000 people are buried in the cemetery. In 1989, it was also discovered that the cemetery had been horribly mismanaged, with graves being reused and carelessly excavated. With such disrespect for the dead, it's no wonder the spirits at the site are restless. Visitors have heard voices and footsteps and seen ghostly figures wandering the grounds.

Louisiana

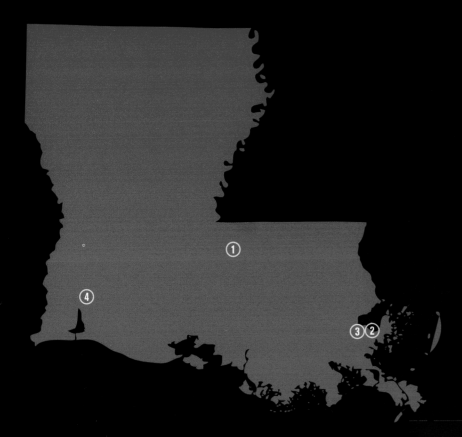

2. (Above) St. Roch Chapel, Yellow Fever Shrine (New Orleans)

In the mid-1800s, as a yellow fever outbreak ravaged New Orleans, the reverend of a local parish began praying to Saint Roch, the patron saint of good health. Not one member of the parish died in the outbreak, and in 1875, the cornerstone of the St. Roch Chapel was laid in honor of the saint's protection. But despite the happy history of this location, it is still known for the spirits that roam the chapel's adjacent cemetery, including a hooded man who seems to walk through walls and a ghostly black dog.

1. (Right) The Myrtles Plantation (St. Francisville)

This historic antebellum plantation was built in the late 1790s over an apparent Tunican burial ground. In recent years, guests have captured photographic evidence of ghosts floating around the home. Ghost experts say as many as a dozen ghosts haunt the plantation; some of those ghosts may be the spirits of those murdered on the grounds. The plantation is currently a bed and breakfast.

3. (Right) LaLaurie Mansion (New Orleans)

The LaLaurie Mansion sits on the site of the original home of Delphine LaLaurie, a socialite known to have tortured and killed many slaves. When LaLaurie's atrocious deeds became public, an angry mob sacked and burned the house. It was rebuilt by a new owner in 1838, but the darkness of what happened on this site continues to linger. For a time, the building served as a girl's school, where students would report being scratched by invisible entities. Today, visitors often hear moans and footsteps in the house.

4. (Left) Calcasieu Courthouse (Lake Charles)

In 1942, convicted murderer Toni Jo Henry became the only woman to ever be executed by electric chair in Louisiana. The execution was carried out at the Calcasieu Courthouse in Lake Charles. Today, almost 80 years later, courthouse workers say they can still feel the presence of Henry in the building. Doors lock on their own, lights flicker, and electronic equipment turns on and off. Some have heard footsteps, whispers or screams. Others are convinced they can smell burning hair, or the scent of Henry's 1940's-era perfume.

Louisiana

6. (Above) Magnolia Plantation (Derry)

This former cotton plantation, a National Historic Landmark, appears today much like it did in the nineteenth century. It's also thought to be haunted by the slaves that once worked there under bondage. Footsteps, odd noises, and creepy figures that resemble soldiers have been reported by guests and museum employees.

5. Muriel's Restaurant (New Orleans)

Muriel's Restaurant in New Orleans has a history spanning back almost to the very year the city was founded, 1718. Over the years, the building at this site was used for family homes, a saloon, a grocery store, and finally, a restaurant. With such a long history, it comes as no surprise that patrons and staff often report ghostly activity, including glasses flying off shelves, voices in empty rooms, and a glowing mist that wanders throughout the lounge.

7. The Mortuary Haunted House (New Orleans)

Considered to be one of the most popular haunted houses in Louisiana, this Greek Revival mansion is a downright spooky spot. The mansion, which is located next to a cemetery, was once a prominent funeral home. Today, guests can tour the home and all of its creepy attractions, including zombies, ghosts, and other paranormal sights and sounds.

8. (Right)
Shreveport Municipal Auditorium (Shreveport)

Built as a memorial to the servicemen of World War I, Shreveport Municipal Auditorium was completed in 1929. The auditorium is best-known for hosting the radio program Louisiana Hayride from 1948 to 1960, which helped launch the careers of artists like Hank Williams, Johnny Cash, and Elvis Presley. In fact, some are convinced that the ghost of Elvis and a few other spirits still visit the building. Doors are known to open and close on their own, voices are heard, and some visitors have seen the apparition of a girl in a blue dress.

9. (Left) Jean Lafitte's Old Absinthe House (New Orleans)

10. Faulkner House Books (New Orleans)

Maine

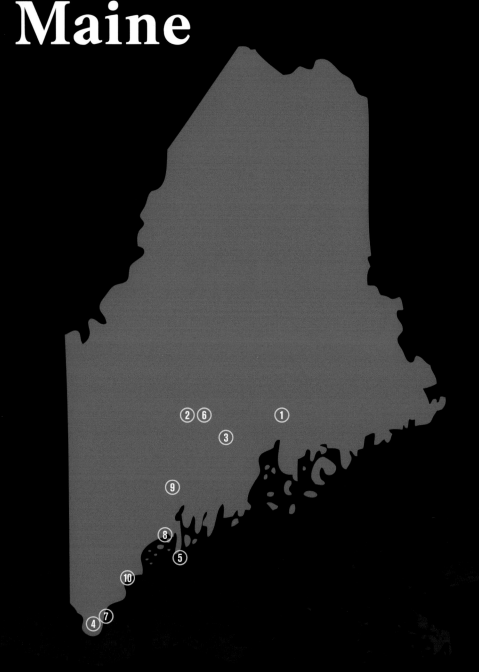

2. Strand Cinema (Skowhegan)

A fixture in the community of Skowhegan since 1929, Strand Cinema is popular for its restored auditorium and reasonable movie prices. But it's also popular for its resident ghost. According to legend, in 1978, a woman died in her apartment above the theater and her spirit never left. During a renovation at the theater that year, worker tools were moved, stains appeared on freshly painted walls, and wallpaper began peeling. Even today, patrons report seeing a woman out of the corner of their eye, only to find she's disappeared when they turn to look at her.

3. Footless Ghost of Benton Falls (Benton)

In 1970, the Linnell family of Benton Falls was renovating the dining room of their eighteenth century house. They made a startling discovery behind a wall: a mummified, shriveled human foot. And that was just the beginning of the strange happenings in the house. Family members reported noises, smells, and shadowy figures lurking in corners. The family's teenaged son felt a presence sitting on his bed one night. Strange footsteps, as if someone with only one foot were walking, were also heard throughout the house.

4. Old York Burying Ground (York)

The graves in the Old Burying Yard span a timeline from 1705 to the 1850s. As with most old cemeteries, the graveyard comes with its fair share of ghost stories. But none is more famous than that of Mary Nasson, who died in 1774. Unlike other graves in the area, Mary's is covered with a heavy stone slab. According to rumor, this is to keep Mary, who was said to be a witch, from rising from the grave. But it hasn't stopped her ghost from appearing from time to time wandering the grounds.

5. Outer Heron Island

More than 3000 islands lie off the coast of Maine. Some are well-populated, some are known for their lighthouses, and some, like Outer Heron Island, are known for their mysteries. For more than a hundred years, rumors have swirled that Aztec treasure is buried on the island. Those who have come to the uninhabited island to search for it have found a cave inscribed with strange drawings, and visitors even sometimes hear a terrifying moaning within the cave. Many believe it is the voice of a protective ghost, guarding the treasure.

6. Lake George Regional Park West (Skowgegan)

This seemingly tranquil public park is a paranormal activity hotspot. Park patrons have reported unusual apparitions, objects on picnic tables being rearranged, and mysterious foggy windows in a park cabin.

7. Museums of Old York (York)

This pre-Revolutionary War settlement transports visitors back in time to a quaint Colonial America. It's also where guests have encountered a dreadful "White Witch," the supposed spirit of a woman once accused of witchcraft. Moving objects, cold spots, and other creepy oddities are not uncommon on this settlement's grounds.

8. Jameson Tavern (Freeport)

9. Old Narrow Gauge Trail (Randolph)

1. Mount Hope Cemetery (Bangor)

Established in 1834, Bangor's Mount Hope Cemetery is the second oldest garden cemetery in the country. The site is the final resting place of Hannibal Hamlin, a politician who served as vice president under Abraham Lincoln, as well as numerous congressmen and governors. It is said that Maine native Stephen King often visited the cemetery during his college years to find spooky story inspiration. And with a reputation for being the most haunted location in Maine, it's no wonder. Just before closing, visitors often hear voices and footsteps echoing through the grounds.

10. (Above) Wood Island Lighthouse (Saco Bay)

Originally built in 1808 at the request of President Thomas Jefferson, this lighthouse was later the site of a murder and a suicide in the late nineteenth century. Lighthouse employees have reported paranormal occurrences like mysterious shadows, unsettling moaning noises, and even gunshots.

Maryland

1. (Above) Point Lookout State Park (Scotland)

This 530-acre park was once a Union prisoner camp during the Civil War; historians say more than 4,000 Confederate soldiers died on its grounds. A lighthouse on the grounds is reportedly haunted by many ghostly spirits who perished during the war. Park visitors continuously report all kinds of supernatural experiences, including spooky voices, shadowy figures, and even peculiar smells.

2. Horse You Came In On Saloon (Baltimore)

On October 3, 1849, writer Edgar Allan Poe was discovered deliriously wandering the streets of Baltimore. Many believe his last stop that night was a bar now dubbed The Horse You Came In On Saloon. And after he died four days later, he may have never left. Staff at "The Horse," as it's often known, report swinging chandeliers and cash registers flying open for no reason. In honor of Poe, the staff will often leave a glass of whiskey on the bar at closing time.

3. (Left) Historic Savage Mill (Savage)

Once a cotton mill complex, the Historic Savage Mill now houses shops, art galleries and restaurants. Visitors can not only browse through shops, but they can take ghost tours, too. The mill is said to be haunted by the ghosts of both adult and child workers, who led difficult lives toiling in the mill. Shop owners often hear children running up and down the halls as they close their stores for the night, and the ghost of a female worker has been known to appear in the men's bathroom!

4. Dr. Samuel A. Mudd House (Waldorf)

Also known as St. Catharine, the Dr. Samuel A. Mudd House is named after Maryland's famous physician. Mudd famously treated an injured John Wilkes Booth the night he assassinated Abraham Lincoln. Many believe that Booth comes back to visit the house every night to rest, just as he did on the night of his crime. No matter how carefully museum staff make up the bed in the so-called "Booth Room", the impression of a human can often be seen in the bed by morning.

Maryland

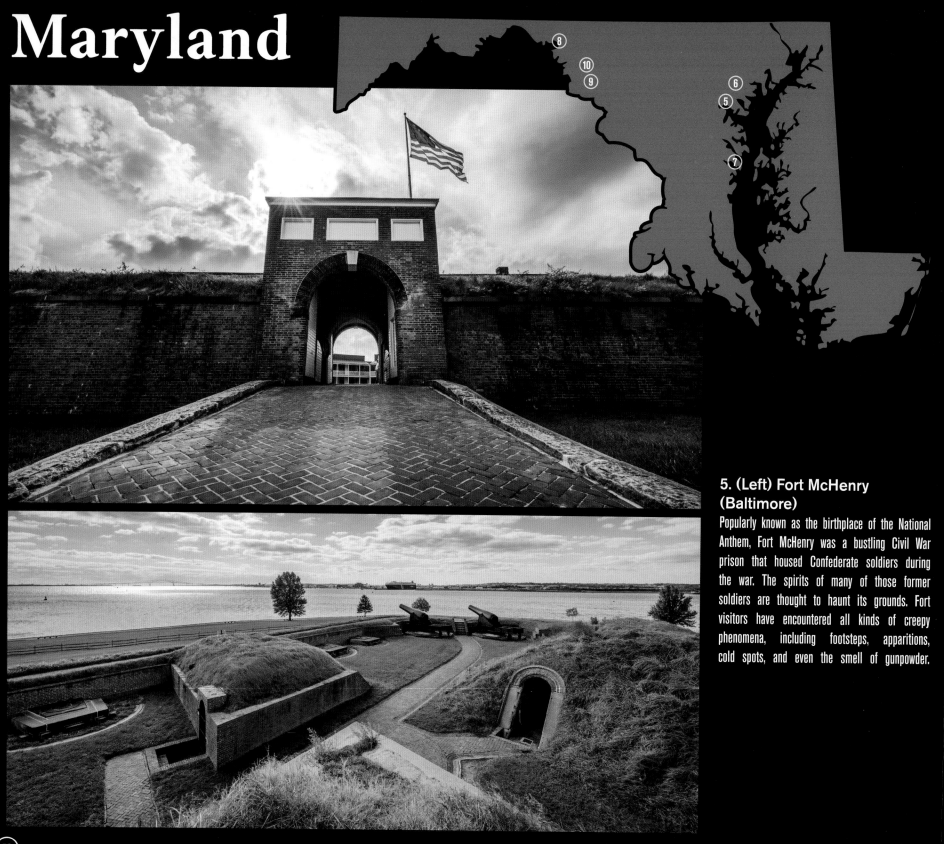

5. (Left) Fort McHenry (Baltimore)

Popularly known as the birthplace of the National Anthem, Fort McHenry was a bustling Civil War prison that housed Confederate soldiers during the war. The spirits of many of those former soldiers are thought to haunt its grounds. Fort visitors have encountered all kinds of creepy phenomena, including footsteps, apparitions, cold spots, and even the smell of gunpowder.

8. (Above) Chesapeake and Ohio Canal (Central Maryland)

9. Coffin Rock (Burkittsville)

6. (Above) Jericho Covered Bridge (Kingsville)

Constructed in 1865, the Jericho Covered Bridge near Kingsville spans the Little Gunpowder Falls River. The 88-foot-long bridge is open to vehicle traffic; it was listed in the National Register of Historic Places in 1978. The historic bridge also has a reputation for being haunted. Cars have been known to inexplicably stall on the bridge late at night, and some motorists say handprints appear on their cars after they drive through the area. Perhaps most chilling, drivers have seen the ghostly silhouettes of people hanging from the bridge's rafters as they drive across.

7. Witch's Grave (Annapolis)

Legend says a witch was once hanged in modern-day Truxton Park. After her burial in the woods, the witch supposedly left her grave and sought revenge on her executioners. On each Halloween night, the spirits of her executioners can be seen hanging from one of the park's trees.

10. (Above) Antietam National Battlefield (Sharpsburg)

Antietam National Battlefield commemorates the Battle of Antietam; the Civil War battle was fought on September 17, 1862. The battle is still considered the bloodiest day in American history, where 25 percent of Union troops and 31 percent of Confederate troops were wounded, captured, or killed in the span of 12 hours. Perhaps it is unsurprising, then, that the area is believed to be haunted. Visitors have seen ghostly blue orbs, heard drums and singing and gunshots, and seen the apparitions of uniformed soldiers wandering the grounds.

Massachusetts

1. Bridgewater Triangle (Southeastern Massachusetts)

This roughly 200-square-mile area in southeastern Massachusetts has been the site of plentiful supernatural activity. Witnesses have reported sightings of UFOs, fire balls, mysterious orbs, and even Bigfoot!

2. (Left) Lizzie Borden Bed & Breakfast (Fall River)

On the morning of August 4, 1892, someone attacked Andrew and Abby Borden in their home in Fall River, Massachusetts, killing them with a hatchet. Andrew's daughter, Lizzie, was accused of murdering her father and stepmother, but she was later acquitted. The house where the crime occurred is now a bed and breakfast, where ghost hunters flock to search for paranormal activity. Some guests have seen ghostly mists or felt a presence sit on their bed. Staff in the house say that the fire alarm sometimes goes off for no reason, always around 3:00 a.m.

3. (Above and Below) House of the Seven Gables (Salem)

Also called the Turner-Ingersoll Mansion, the House of the Seven Gables in Salem was made famous by Nathaniel Hawthorne's novel of the same name. Named for its triangular, gabled roof, the house was originally built in 1668, with additions added in the eighteenth century. A longtime fixture in a town famous for its witch trials, the house is believed by many who visit to be haunted. Ghostly figures have been seen on staircases and peering through windows, and guests often hear voices and footsteps.

4. (Above and Below) USS *Salem* (Quincy Harbor)

This commanding Cold War-era heavy cruiser today calls Quincy home. She sailed around the world in the 1950s following her commission in 1949. Eerily well-preserved, the USS *Salem* is surprisingly spooky; guests have heard footsteps, voices, and loud banging noises during tours.

Massachusetts

5. (Above and Left) King's Chapel Burying Ground (Boston)

As the oldest graveyard in Boston, the King's Chapel Burying Ground is featured on the city's famous Freedom Trail. The graveyard, established in 1630, is the final resting place of many prominent Massachusetts colonists, including Mary Chilton, the first European woman to set foot in New England. Unsurprisingly, this historic graveyard comes with its fair share of ghosts. Many have seen glowing orbs and heard voices on the grounds, but perhaps most disturbing are the occasional muffled screams that seem to emanate from the graves.

6. (Above and Below) Hawthorne Hotel (Salem)

An elevator and the sixth floor are considered haunted in this downright creepy hotel, which was named after author Nathaniel Hawthorne. Historians say a double murder occurred on the hotel's grounds; guests have felt cold spots, reported moving furniture, and even seen sightings of a ghostly woman.

7. (Portrait of Jenny Lind, Above) Jenny Lind Tower (Boston)

In 1850, renowned opera singer Jenny Lind was performing for an oversold audience in an auditorium in Boston. Crowds of people, unable to get in, began to crash the gates, and Lind climbed a tower in the building and sang to the crowds below. When the building was torn down in 1927, the tower, now called Jenny Lind Tower, was moved to North Truro on Cape Cod. The area is said to be haunted by a banshee, whose screams can be heard at sunset. But Lind continues to enchant, her ghost climbing the tower and driving away the banshee with song.

8. Lyceum Hall (Salem)

On February 12, 1877, inventor Alexander Graham Bell stunned observers at Salem's Lyceum Hall when he made a phone call to his assistant in Boston. The building where Bell made history, which now houses a restaurant, was built on the site of a former apple orchard. The orchard was owned by Bridget Bishop, the first woman to be executed for witchcraft during the Salem Witch Trials. Many believe Bridget's ghost now haunts the building, where objects fly off shelves and the scent of apples lingers. Some also see the ghost staring at them in reflections in mirrors, window panes, or light fixtures.

9. Ropes Mansion (Salem)

10. Joshua Ward House (Salem)

Michigan

1. Henderson Castle (Kalamazoo)

Henderson Castle sits on a hill overlooking downtown Kalamazoo. It was built in 1895 by Frank Henderson, one of Kalamazoo's most successful businessmen. Henderson's 25-room house included seven bathrooms, a ballroom, and an elevator, but he was only able to enjoy the home for four years before he died in 1899. Many guests believe that Frank and his wife, Mary, continue to haunt the house. Visitors and staff have seen apparitions, heard voices and doors slamming, and have felt a presence walk by on the staircase.

2. (Above) South Manitou Island

Located just west of Leland, South Manitou Island is accessible by ferry and popular with hikers and campers. Although it is currently uninhabited, save for a few park rangers during summer months, the island was home to many farming families in the 1800s; it still contains abandoned buildings and a cemetery that hint at the island's once-thriving past. But the rangers who stay on the island often hear footsteps and voices in the abandoned buildings, and some have seen the spirit of a woman who wanders the lonely shore with a lantern.

4. (Above and Below) The Masonic (Detroit)

Often referred to simply as "The Masonic," the Detroit Masonic Temple is the largest Masonic temple in the world, encompassing 16 floors and 1,037 rooms. The structure contains public spaces like theaters and banquet halls; it also includes a swimming pool, gym, and bowling alley. Completed in 1926, the entire structure was designed by architect George D. Mason, who is now said to haunt his creation. Many guests claim to have seen Mason in the vast halls, and visitors report cold spots, slamming doors, and a feeling of being watched.

3. (Above and Below) Traverse City State Hospital (Traverse City)

Constructed in the late nineteenth century, the Traverse City State Hospital once housed several thousand patients in its facilities. The site was ultimately added to the National Register of Historic Places in 1978 before the hospital's closure in 1989. Multiple types of paranormal activity has been reported on the hospital's grounds, including unusual voices and footsteps, mysterious lights, and random temperature changes.

Michigan

5. The Paulding Light (Paulding)
First reported in the 1960s, the Paulding Light continues to spook onlookers. The mysterious light—bright, white, and known to change in size and shape—appears in a valley outside of Paulding. Locals, researchers, and ghost hunters offer all kinds of explanations about the creepy phenomenon, ranging from gas, geological activity, to ghosts. No matter the case, the light is definitely unnerving.

6. (Above) Seul Choix Point Lighthouse (Gulliver)
Located in the only harbor in a treacherous stretch of coastline along Lake Michigan near Gulliver, the French name of the Seul Choix Point Lighthouse fittingly means "only choice." Completed in 1892 and automated in 1972, the site is now open to the public for tours. Visitors often come searching for the ghost of Captain Joseph Townsend, a cigar-smoking keeper who died in the lighthouse in 1910. Some have seen a figure peering out of an upstairs window when the lighthouse is empty, and many guests report smelling cigar smoke.

7. (Right) Felt Mansion (Saugatuck)

Dorr and Agnes Felt purchased this sprawling mansion in 1928. Unfortunately, Anges died six weeks after the couple moved into the home. Some say Agnes never left, as visitors to the home have experienced items mysteriously moving, doors and windows randomly closing, and an apparition roaming the third floor.

8. (Left) River Raisin National Battlefield Park (Monroe)

The only national battlefield to mark a site of the War of 1812, the River Raisin National Battlefield Park commemorates the Battle of Frenchtown; the battle took place in January 1813. It was a devastating loss for the American soldiers, and many of the survivors were later killed by members of the Potawatomi tribe. The violent history of the site has led to many ghost sightings, including glowing lights and apparitions of soldiers. Many visitors also report hearing voices and screams.

9. Doherty Hotel (Clare)

10. The Whitney Restaurant (Detroit)

Minnesota

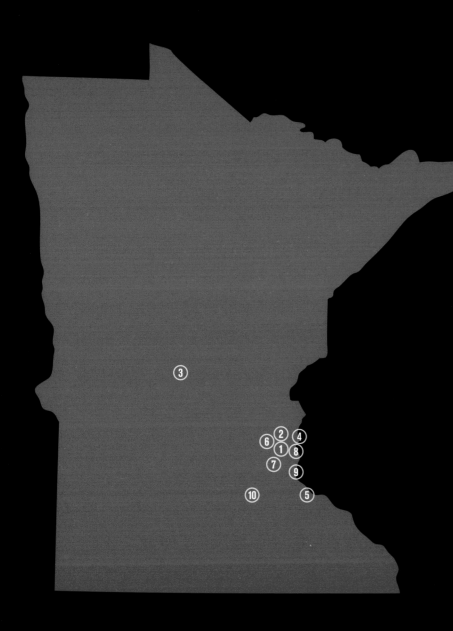

2. (Above) Burbank Livingston Griggs House (St. Paul)

Designed in an Italianate style by architect Otis L. Wheelock, the Burbank Livingston Griggs House was built in 1862. The house is named after three of its early owners who were influential in the development of Minnesota's capital city. The house has now been converted into three rentable apartments, but tenants should be aware that the mansion is considered the most haunted house in the city! The apparitions of a maid, gardener, and at least two former owners have been spotted in the mansion, along with several other ghostly entities.

3. (Above) Palmer House Hotel (Sauk Centre)

Located in Sauk Centre, the Palmer House Hotel is located on the site of the first hotel in the city, which burned down in 1900. The current hotel was built one year later by Ralph and Christena Palmer. The hotel was the first building in the city to have electricity, giving it a reputation for modernity and elegance. But today, the hotel is better known for its ghosts. Guests have reported hearing knocks on their doors in the middle of the night, seeing ghostly apparitions, and hearing empty chairs creak and groan.

1. Wabasha Street Caves (St. Paul)

The Wabasha Street Caves in Saint Paul are technically "mines" since the sandstone caves were man-made. Dating back to the 1840s, the caves have been used for everything from storage space to speakeasies; the caves suppoedly welcomed mobsters and gangsters in the 1920s. Some of these gangsters are said to haunt the space today, which is now used as an event hall. Patrons have reported seeing apparitions of men in 1920s attire and shadowy figures on the dance floor.

6. Mounds Theatre (St. Paul)

The apparition of a little girl supposedly haunts this early twentieth century theatre—and she's not the theatre's on paranormal oddity. Located on St. Paul's east side, this playhouse is also the site of a creepy projection booth ar spooky basement. In fact, investigators reported claw marks on their backs after touring the theatre's basemen

7. Father Hennepin Bluffs Park (Minneapolis)

Father Hennepin Bluff Park in Minneapolis, is named after Franciscan priest Father Louis Hennepin, who led a expedition through the area in 1680. An oasis in the middle of the city, the 5.5-acre park sits on a bluff wit views of the Mississippi River. The park is located in the Saint Anthony Main neighborhood, which is considere the most haunted area of the city. Legend has it a Native American burial ground was destroyed when the par was created, and angry spirits linger. Those who visit the park say it has an ominous feeling, even during the da

4. (Above) Warden's House Museum (Stillwater)

Originally part of the Minnesota Territorial Prison, the Warden's House Museum in Stillwater was the home of the prison's wardens from 1853 to 1914. After the prison closed in 1914, the house served as a home or other officials, until the Washington County Historical Society took ownership in 1941. Today, the house s the only museum in the city, and it is said to be haunted by several ghosts. The most famous is a woman named Trudy, who sometimes appears in the master bedroom or can be seen gazing from upstairs windows.

8. (Above) Schmidt Brewery Building (St. Paul)

Currently home to revitalized lofts, the old Schmidt Brewery building is famous for its crenellate towers and Gothic looks. But back in the early twentieth century, it was where multiple brewer workers died horrible deaths, including in explosions, elevator shaft falls, and other grisly disasters Legend says some of the departed spirits haunt the old building's grounds nearly 100 years later

9. Grey Cloud Island Township

10. Crazy Annie's Bridge (Henderson)

5. (Above) St. James Hotel (Red Wing)

A handful of ghosts haunt this historic hotel, including a woman in a white dress, a workman, and an angry apparition. Hotel staff and former guests claim that the third floor is particularly spooky; the floor's Room 310 is the room of former owner Clara Lillyblad. Unusual voices, cold

Mississippi

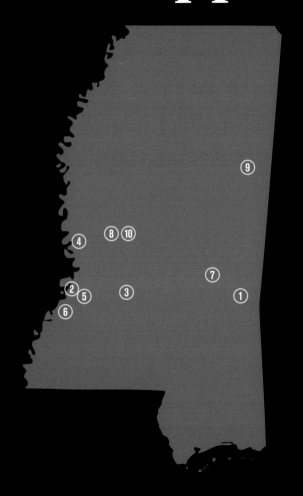

1. Grand Opera House (Meridian)

The Grand Opera House in Meridian is also known as the Mississippi State University Riley Center. The opera house opened in 1890 and enjoyed several decades of popularity, until it was converted to a movie theater in 1920. The Great Depression forced it to close, but a restoration project in 2000 uncovered the building's original grandeur. The site is believed to come with its own "phantom of the opera," which has been known to touch people on the shoulder. Visitors also often complain of random cold spots throughout the building.

2. McRaven House (Vicksburg)

The first section of the McRaven House in Vicksburg was built in 1797 as a way station for travelers on the Natchez Trace. Additions were made to the house in 1836 and 1849, but it fell into disrepair by the 1960s. After restoration projects, the house was opened to the public, for historical and ghost tours. Several people have died in the house over the centuries, and their spirits are said to linger on the property.

3. (Above) University of Mississippi Medical Center (Jackson)

Construction crews have discovered thousands of bodies on the grounds of the former Mississippi State Asylum, a facility that predated Jackson's modern-day Medical Center. During its eight decades of operation the asylum treated tens of thousands of people; however, nearly 9,000 patients died at the former facility. Some locals are convinced that the spirits of those deceased patients roam the university's medical campus.

4. Mont Helena (Rolling Fork)

Built atop a ceremonial Indian mound and surrounded by vast cornfields, Rolling Fork's Mont Helena is an unusual mansion. The home was built in 1896 by Helen and George Harris, on land left to them by Helen's father, who called it "the Helen Place." Helen and George lived out their days at Mont Helena, and some believe they never left. The house is open for tours, and many visitors report hearing footsteps and voices, or find unexplainable orbs in their photos. Others have seen a woman in a white gown, believed to be Helen herself.

5. (Above and Below) Vicksburg National Military Park (Vicksburg)

This Mississippi site was where one of the Civil War's most brutal battles occurred. Today, it's known for its deceptively tranquil hills and quaint greenery; it's also home to some downright creepy paranormal activity. Park patrons have supposedly heard cannon fire and shouting soldiers. Other visitors have smelled gunpowder, spotted the apparitions of Civil War soldiers, and witnessed the faces of soldiers on a monument crying blood.

6. (Above) Windsor Ruins (Port Gibson)

7. Stuckey's Bridge (Union)

Although no one is certain of its exact date of construction, Stuckey's Bridge is believed to have been built around 1850. The iron bridge spans the Chunky River, and was added to the National Register of Historic Places in 1988. Legend says that "Stuckey" was a robber and murderer who was a member of the infamous Dalton Gang. When he was apprehended, he was hanged from the bridge. Now, many say that Stuckey's ghost haunts the bridge, his lifeless, hanging form appearing as a ghostly apparition.

8. Witch of Yazoo Grave Site (Yazoo City)

According to legend, in 1884 an old woman lived on the Yazoo River in Mississippi who would capture and torture fishermen. When the local sheriff questioned her, she fled and got caught in quicksand. As she sank to her death, she vowed to return in 20 years and burn Yazoo City to the ground. She was buried in Glenwood Cemetery, and a chain was placed around the gravesite to prevent her spirit from leaving. Exactly 20 years later, a great fire tore through the city. When locals checked the "witch's" grave, the chain links were broken.

9. Friendship Cemetery (Columbus)

This ominous cemetery is home to Confederate soldier graves, including many who fought in 1862's Battle of Shiloh. Legend says the spirits of those soldiers keep watch at night.

10. Satartia Bridge (Yazoo City)

Missouri

3. Zombie Road (Wildwood)
Lawler Ford Road in Wildwood was constructed in the 1860s to create access to the Meramec River. Less a true "road" and more a trail, the two-mile-long, 10-foot-wide path is better known by its nickname, "Zombie Road." Legends tell of a "zombie killer" who lived in a shack by the trail, and some believe he still haunts the area today. Other sightings on the road include the ghosts of Native Americans, Civil War soldiers, and children. But the most common reports are of shadowy, humanoid shapes that follow travelers down the trail.

1. Savoy Hotel (Kansas City)
Built in 1888, the Savoy Hotel in Kansas City was originally frequented by travelers arriving at the nearby Union Depot train station. Until 2016, it was the oldest continuously operating hotel in the U.S. west of the Mississippi River, but recent renovations have given it a more modern flair. Despite its contemporary feel, guests believe that ghosts of the past remain within its walls. Many have reported footsteps, water faucets and radios turning on and off, and the sound of closing doors. Some guests have even seen apparitions in their rooms.

2. Lemp Mansion (St. Louis)
Built in the 1860s, the Lemp Mansion was purchased by beer brewer William J. Lemp as a family home. Lemp's father, John, is considered to be the country's first lager beer brewer, and his business made the Lemps one of the wealthiest families in the city. But their wealth couldn't protect them from tragedy; several members of the family died in the house, including William, who died by suicide. Now a restaurant and inn, staff and guests often report strange occurrences, including doors locking and unlocking on their own, voices, apparitions, and phantom piano music.

4. (Above) 1836 Missouri State Penitentiary (Jefferson City)
Until it was decommissioned in 2004, the Missouri State Penitentiary in Jefferson City was the oldest continually operating prison west of the Mississippi River. Opened in 1836, the prison housed inmates for 168 years, including the killer of Martin Luther King Jr., James Earl Ray, who escaped from the prison a year before the assassination. With a long history of riots, murders, and executions, it's no surprise that this prison is considered to be haunted. Visitors have been touched by ghostly hands, seen shadowy apparitions, and heard cell doors slamming.

5. (Above) Pythian Castle (Springfield)

This 40,000-square-foot mansion was built in the 1910s as a home for widows and orphans of the Knights of Pythias, a fraternal organization. In World War II, the United States military used the mansion for troop rehabilitation. Today, it's a popular spot for ghost hunting.

6. Beattie Mansion (St. Joseph)

Armstrong and Eliza Beattie built this curious mansion in the 1850s. After their deaths in 1878 and 1880, the mansion was converted into a home for the sick and eldery. By the late twentieth century, the mansion served as a group home for the mentally ill. Developers later purchased the mansion in 2004 with the intention to turn it into a bed and breakfast; during its renovation, contractors reported hearing spooky voices and seeing shadowy apparitions. Ghost hunters say the mansion's original owners now haunt the home.

7. Vaile Mansion (Independence)

Located in Independence, the Vaile Mansion was built in 1881 for wealthy businessman Harvey M. Vaile, who lived in the house until his death in 1895. The opulent home has since been used as a sanatorium, a nursing home, and even a water bottling company; today, it is open to the public for tours. Guests often report ghostly sightings, especially of Vaile's wife, Sophia, who died by suicide in the home in 1883. Her white-gowned apparition is sometimes seen roaming the halls or peering out of an upstairs bedroom window.

8. Maine Street (St. Charles)

9. Union Station (St. Louis)

10. (Above and Below) The Governor's Mansion (Jefferson City)

Missouri's Governor's Mansion is one of the oldest governor's mansions in the country. Completed in 1871, it has been the home of the state's sitting governor since 1872. In the 1880s, Thomas Chittenden's 10-year-old daughter died in the mansion from diphtheria. During renovation work more than 100 years later, a repairman reportedly heard a little girl playing in the home; he later asked a housekeeper about the girl's identity. The housekeeper said that there was no else in the mansion, and the repairman promptly fled the home.

Montana

1. (Below) The Fairweather Inn (Virginia City)

First opened in 1863, the Fairweather Inn is located in the former gold mining town of Virginia City. In the late nineteenth century, the town was a boomtown filled with thousands of prospectors, and it was even the site of Montana's first public school. But once the gold was gone, Virginia City became a ghost town, and the Fairweather Inn is said to be home to many spirits. Guests have heard whispers and footsteps in the middle of the night, and some have found their room doors inexplicably unlocked in the morning!

2. (Above and Below) Little Bighorn Battlefield (Crow Agency)

Commonly referred to as "Custer's Last Stand," the 1867 Battle of the Little Bighorn was fought between the 7th Cavalry Regiment of the United States Army and Lakota, Northern Cheyenne, and Arapaho tribes near what is now Crow Agency. The battle was a major defeat for the U.S. Army, resulting in the death of Lieutenant Colonel George Armstrong Custer and 267 other soldiers. Today, the site contains a mass grave of those who died; visitors regularly report seeing the restless spirits of both U.S. soldiers and Native Americans wandering the battlefield.

3. (Above and Below) Garnet Ghost Town (Drummond)

The Garnet Ghost Town in Drummond is considered the state's best preserved ghost town. Dating back to 1895, the town was named for the ruby-colored, semi-precious stones found in the mines nearby, yet gold was the main draw for the prospectors who came to the town. But only ten years later, the mining began to dwindle; Garnet was a ghost town by the 1940s. Today, it draws ghost hunters, who say Kelly's Saloon is the most haunted building in town. The sounds of music, laughter, and slamming doors are often heard in the empty building.

Montana

4. (Below) Old Montana Prison (Deer Lodge)

Built by convict labor in the 1800s, the Old Montana Prison is now part of a museum complex in Deer Lodge. The prison began housing convicts in 1871, and it quickly earned a reputation for being overcrowded and poorly managed. The site of unrest and violence, including a major riot in 1959, the prison was closed in 1979 and reopened as a museum in 1980. But many believe the riot had a lasting effect, stranding spirits within the prison walls. Visitors have heard screams, seen glowing orbs, and heard footsteps in empty cells.

5. (Above) Many Glacier Hotel (Browning)

Glacier National Park, located in northeastern Montana, is sometimes called "the Switzerland of North America." Visitors from around the world come to see the snow-capped Rocky Mountains and hike and camp in the park. Those who don't feel like roughing it often choose to stay at the Many Glacier Hotel, a five-story hotel on the shores of Swiftcurrent Lake. But park visitors sometimes find they aren't the only guests at the hotel. One visitor saw the ghost of a woman in a red dress in his room; others have seen apparitions vanish before their eyes.

6. Boulder Hot Springs Hotel (Boulder)

Boulder's famous inn was built in the early 1880s as a resting spot for ranchers and miners. Guests of the inn today regularly come into contact with all kinds of ghosts, including the spirit of a murdered prostitute named Simone. Visitors consistently witness other paranormal oddities, including cold spots and mysterious noises, during their stays at this creepy spot.

7. Fort Peck Theatre (Fort Peck)

This creepy theatre opened in the 1930s around the time of the construction of the Fort Peck Dam. The theatre was used for entertainment, including theatrical productions, as well as for housing U.S. Army Corps of Engineers employees and their families. Today, the building is supposedly haunted by the spirit of a man dressed in the 1930s work attire; guests have also heard noises that resemble men working.

8. The Pollard Hotel (Red Lodge)

This brick building was built in the 1890s; after its purchase by Thomas F. Pollard, the building was turned into a hotel. Over the years, hotel staff and guests have encountered apparitions, including a man dressed in 1920s-era apparel and a woman in a yellow dress.

9. Daly Mansion (Hamilton)

10. Grand Union Hotel (Fort Benton)

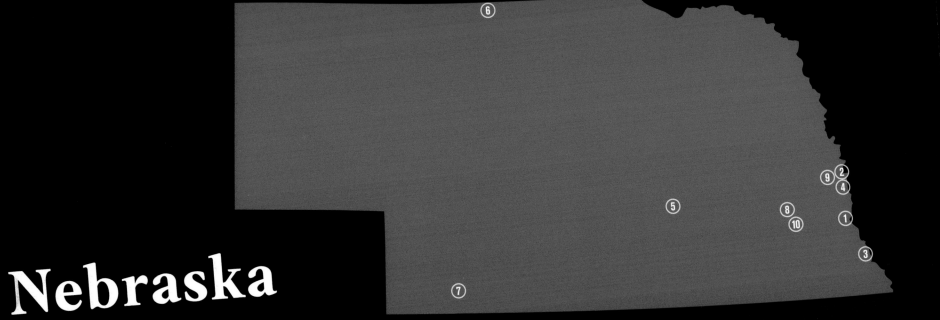

Nebraska

1. Seven Sisters Road (Otoe County)
According to legend, in the early 1900s a family of seven sisters and one brother lived off a winding road in Otoe County near seven hills. After a terrible argument one night, the brother lured each sister to a different hill and hanged them from trees until they were dead. Today, a street known as Seven Sisters Road meanders through the area, and motorists insist the women's spirits linger nearby. Some have heard screams or seen shadowy figures in the darkness, while others report cars stalling or inexplicably dimming headlights.

2. Annie Cook's Poor Farm (Omaha)
Annie Petsky was born in 1875 and married Nebraskan farmer Frank Cook in 1893, settling in the town of Hershey. Even after their daughter, Clara, was born in 1894, Annie wasn't content with farm life. She secretly started a brothel in Omaha and turned the farm in Hershey into a "poor farm," where destitute men came to work. Annie treated them horribly, working some of them to death. Even worse, in 1934, she killed her own daughter after an argument. The site of the poor farm is said to be haunted, not only by Annie but by many of the victims of her violence.

3. Bailey House Museum (Brownville)
This brick Gothic Revival house was built in the late 1870s. It's said to be haunted by the spirit of Captain Bailey, a former Civil War captain who lived in the home until he was poisoned by a jealous neighbor. Visitors say they have heard a piano playing late at night—despite there being no piano in sight.

4. Hummel Park (Omaha)
This 200-acre park is where people have come to perform satanic rituals and animal sacrifices.

5. Witch's Bridge (Grand Island)
According to local legend, there once was a woman who lived in a house at the end of a bridge who was suspected of practicing witchcraft and devil worship. The townsfolk, desperate to rid themselves of her evil, tied her to a stake and burned both her and her house. Today, the bridge is known as Witch's Bridge, and ghost hunters believe the woman never left. Cars have been known to inexplicably stall on the bridge, and some have seen the apparition of a dog with glowing red eyes.

6. Centennial Hall Museum (Valentine)
Originally used as a school, the Centennial Hall Museum in Valentine was built in 1897. Rumor says that a girl, a clarinetist in the school orchestra, was murdered in 1944 when a classmate poisoned her clarinet reed. Even before the building was converted into a museum, teachers claimed to see the ghostly apparition of the girl in the hallways. Now, visitors to the museum often report hearing music coming from the old music hall, despite the fact that all the instruments were removed long ago.

7. Devil's Canyon (McCook)
Just north of McCook, Nebraska, a dirt road runs up to a lonely canyon. The locals have dubbed it Devil's Canyon because of an old legend about the site. According to the story, more than 100 years ago a man nicknamed "The Duke" brought his wife and children out to the isolated area to murder them; he then died by suicide. Today, visitors to the area say the ghost of The Duke appears as a shadowy figure, roaming the hills, and some even say he torments the dreams of anyone who visits the canyon.

8. Temple Theatre (Lincoln)

9. Mystery Manor (Omaha)

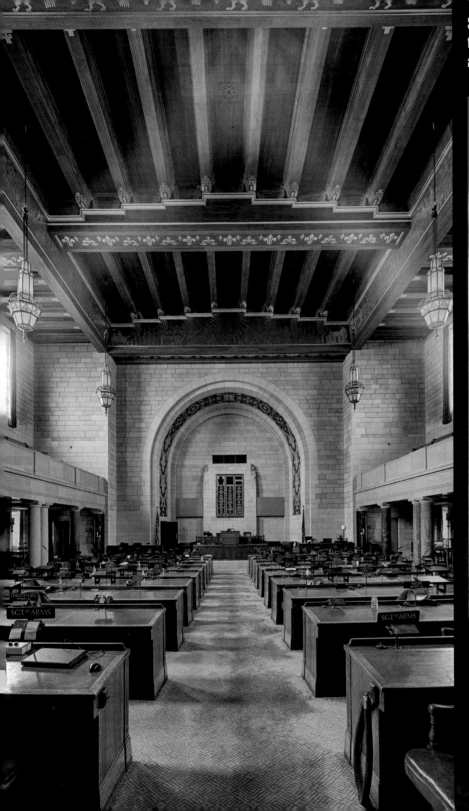

Some believe Nebraska's Capitol Building was constructed on holy Native American land. Since its opening the building has been the site of multiple grisly deaths, many of them accidents. Today, guests report seeing apparitions roaming the building; others have heard mysterious sounds like screams, cries, and footsteps

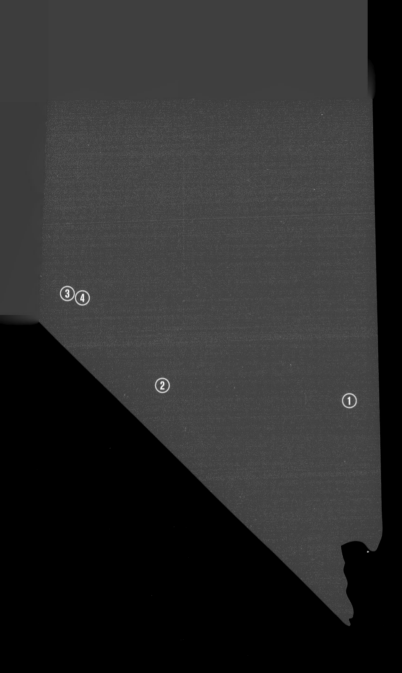

③ ④

②

①

2. (Above and Below) The Clown Motel (Tonopah)

The Clown Motel in Tonopah is exactly what it sounds like—a motel filled with thousands of clown statues figurines, dolls, and wall hangings. Built in 1985 by siblings Leona and Leroy David, the motel was created in hono of their father, Clarence, who died in a mine fire. Fittingly, Clarence was buried in the now-abandoned cemeter that sits next door to the motel. As if a motel filled with clowns next to a cemetery wasn't creepy enough, guests also complain of lights turning on and off in the middle of the night and of belongings being moved or hidden

Boot Hill Cemetery (Pioche)

small, quaint town of Pioche is a peaceful home to around 1,000 people. But in the 1870s, it
a silver mining boomtown known for its gunfights. In fact, it is said that between 1871 and
, 60 percent of the homicides in the state were committed in Pioche. And the gunfighters
"died with their boots on" were laid to rest at the local Boot Hill Cemetery. With the town's
ry of violence, it's no wonder that many believe the souls of those in the cemetery are restless

3. (Above) Piper's Opera House (Virginia City)

Piper's Opera House in Virginia City is the third opera house to stand in its location. The first and second, built by John Piper in 1863 and 1878, respectively, both burned down. Piper then built a third venue in 1885, which remains in use today. Entertainers like Houdini, John Phillip Sousa, and Mark Twain all performed on the opera house stage at one time, and the historic building is the source of many ghostly tales. Patrons have seen glowing orbs, felt cold spots, and heard phantom singing.

4. Mackay Mansion (Virginia City)

The Italianate-style mansion was built in the late 1850s and later became the home of silver miner John Mackay. Today, it's known as the home of several ghosts, including a small girl seen by such people as actor Johnny Depp. Orbs, footsteps, and other unusual noises are common occurrences at this historical haunt.

Nevada

5. Mizpah Hotel (Tonopah)

This five-story hotel opened in the early twentieth century during the area's silver rush. It was the state's tallest building at its opening, and it featured a host of popular amenities like cold and hot running water, steam heat, and an electric elevator. More than a century after its opening, the Mizpah is considered indisputably haunted by a mysterious lady in red, a nameless soldier, and a pair of children. Despite its creepiness, the hotel remains a popular hospitality destination.

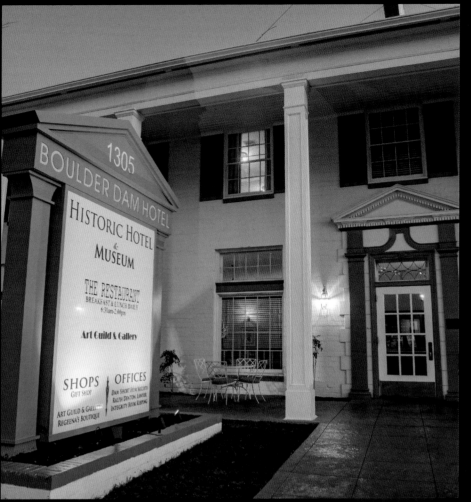

10. (Above and Below) Hoover Dam

Dedicated by President Franklin D. Roosevelt in 1935, Hoover Dam sits on the Colorado River on the border of Nevada and Arizona, where it supplies hydroelectric power over a three-state span. Construction of the dam was a huge undertaking, and more than 100 workers lost their lives from falling, drowning, or other accidents. The dam, which is open for tours, is said to be haunted. Visitors report hearing footsteps and crying, and many have seen apparitions of men in old-fashioned work clothing.

6. (Above) Boulder Dam Hotel (Boulder City)

Built during the construction of the Hoover Dam, the Colonial Revival-style Boulder Dam Hotel is home to plenty of paranormal activity. Employees have heard unusual voices and music originating from the building's ballroom; they've also seen elevator doors that randomly open and close. Guests have reported feeling hands on their shoulders and sensing unusual presences in the hotel's lobby.

7. La Palazza Mansion (Las Vegas)

Unlike some haunted locations, which seem benign and harmless enough, the La Palazza Mansion in Las Vegas has an air of evil about it. According to local legend, the now-abandoned house was once owned by a mobster, who is said to have constructed secret rooms within the walls. Numerous people are rumored to have been murdered in the home, and a former owner even claimed that he was choked by the icy fingers of an angry ghost. Passersby have seen glowing orbs on the property and felt a malevolent energy at the site.

8. Fox Ridge Park (Henderson)

9. Sandhill Road Tunnels (Las Vegas)

New Hampshire

1. (Left and Above) Mount Washington Hotel (Bretton Woods)

Mount Washington Hotel is located in Bretton Woods and was constructed in 1900 by wealthy coal broker Joseph Stickney. After Stickney died in 1903, his wife, Carolyn, continued to live in the hotel; she lived in Room 314. Today, this room, which still contains Carolyn's original bed, is said to be the most haunted room in the hotel. Guests staying in the room have heard loud noises in the middle of the night, smelled perfume, or even awoken to find a woman sitting on the bed, brushing her hair.

3. Pine Hill Cemetery (Hollis)

Mourners buried Abel Blood here in 1867; ever since his burial, Blood has become an infamous ghost. Cemetery patrons have reported all kinds of creepy activity on these grounds, including tapping noises, unusual flashes of light, and cold spots. These paranormal activities have one thing in common: the likely culprit is the spirit of Abel Blood.

4. Amos J. Blake House Museum (Fitzwilliam)

The Amos J. Blake House was built in 1837 as a home and law office for Blake, a state legislator, and his family. The house remained in the Blake family until 1966, when the last living family member gifted the home to the Fitzwilliam Historical Society. The house is now home to not only a museum but several ghosts, too. Some of the most commonly seen spirits are those of a cat and a young boy. Visitors have also heard voices and sleigh bells and seen objects move on their own.

5. Kimball Castle (Gilford)

This two-and-a-half story medieval-style castle, built in 1894, overlooks Lake Winnipesaukee, the largest lake in the state. After falling into disrepair in the 1970s, the property was abandoned, but recent efforts are leading to its restoration. Those who visited the abandoned castle often told tales of strange happenings, including broken antique clocks that would start to tick and lights that flicker on and off.

2. (Above and Below) Madame Sherri Forest (West Chesterfield)

The Madame Sherri Forest is named after eccentric costume designer Madame Antoinette Sherri. In the 1920s, Madame Sherri entertained Broadway elite in her "castle" on the property, but the house burned to the ground in 1962, leaving only a dramatic stone staircase. Madame Sherri died in 1965, but many believe she remains in the forest. Some have seen the figure of a woman in a flowing gown at the top of the staircase, and others say the sounds of music and laughter emanate from the site of the old house.

6. Ocean-Born Mary House (Henniker)

Legend says a pirate captain named Don Pedro captured a ship off of Massachusetts's shore in 1720. The captain pledged to spare the captives' lives so long as a red-haired newborn child onboard was named after his mother, Mary Wallace. Decades later, the now red-haired woman married Don Pedro, and the two lived together in a mansion until he was killed near their property. Following the woman's death in 1814, a red-haired ghost is said to roam the old home.

7. The Tilton Inn (Tilton)

A ghost named Laura reportedly haunts this nineteenth century inn; the spirit is supposedly the ghost of a 12-year-old girl who died in a fire at the site more than 100 years ago.

8. Huntress Hall at Keene State College (Keene)

A residence hall at Keene State College, Huntress Hall is named after a former board of education director named Harriet Huntress. Built in 1926, four years after Huntress died, the dormitory originally housed all-female residents. But during World War II, male naval pilots used the hall during training. They began complaining of creaking, rolling sounds coming from the attic, where Huntress's old wheelchair was stored. Reports of strange noises and even screams have continued to this day, with some believing Huntress disapproves of men in the building.

9. Vale End Cemetery (Wilton)

10. The Chase House (Portsmouth)

New Jersey

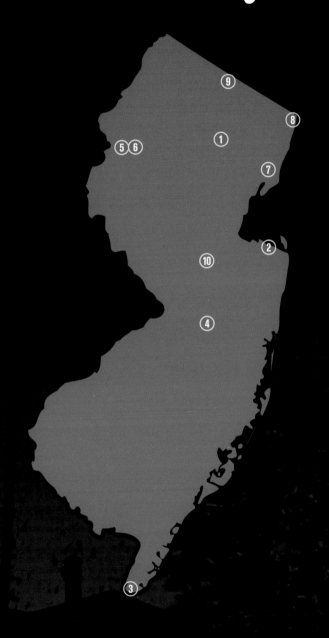

2. (Above and Below) Seabrook-Wilson House (Port Monmouth)

Also known as The Spy House, this coastal home was built in the early eighteenth century and owned by multiple generations of the Seabrook family. By the twentieth century, the property became a boarding house, restaurant, and inn. In the 1960s, a historical society bought the home and turned it into a museum. Rumors say the home was used as a colonial spying post during the Revolutionary War; what's indisputable, locals say, is that the property is a popular spot for ghosts.

1. The Devil's Tree (Basking Ridge)

A lone oak tree that grows in an undeveloped field in Basking Ridge, the Devil's Tree is surrounded by rumor and legend. One story claims that the tree was used by the Ku Klux Klan to lynch slaves; another says that a farmer who lived on the land hanged himself from the tree. Many say the tree is cursed, and anyone who vandalizes or disrespects the tree will experience bad luck or bodily harm—and maybe even something worse. Others say the tree is warm to the touch and insist it is a portal to hell.

5. Shippen Manor (Oxford)

Shippen Manor was constructed on a 4,000-acre estate in Oxford, New Jersey, in 1755. It was the home of Dr. William Shippen II, the founder of the first maternity hospital in America, and his brother, Joseph. The manor was added to the National Register of Historic Places in 1984, and with its centuries of history, it's no surprise that many believe it's haunted. Some have seen apparitions of a Revolutionary-era soldier and a little boy, and visitors report items appearing on shelves that were previously empty.

3. (Above) Emlen Physick Estate (Cape May)

Located in Cape May, the Emlen Physick Estate is an 18-room Victorian mansion, now used as a museum. The mansion was completed in 1879; it was home to Physick as well as his mother and two aunts. By 1935, all members of the family had died, and the house passed to new owners. But it didn't take long for the stories of hauntings to start swirling. Those who have visited, lived in, or worked at the house tell of footsteps, ghostly voices, and doors opening and closing by themselves.

4. (Above) Pine Barrens

Located on the southern side of New Jersey, the Pine Barrens covers more than seven counties in the state. The 1.1 million-acre area was once a popular iron manufacturing location, especially during the Revolutionary War and War of 1812. It's also known for its paranormal activity, including a demonic creature known as the Jersey Devil, ghosts, and animal spirits.

6. (Above) Jenny Jump State Forest (Warren County)

Located in Warren County, New Jersey, Jenny Jump State Forest runs along the 1,129-foot high, six-mile-long Jenny Jump Mountain ridge. According to legend, the forest was named for a young girl named Jenny who lived in the area centuries ago. While on the mountain, she was chased by a Native American man and jumped to her death. Some still see Jenny's spirit floating through the forest. But she isn't the only apparition; visitors also see spirits hovering over Ghost Lake, which is said to cover a Native American burial ground.

7. Snake Hill (Secaucus)

Snake Hill is a rocky slope. From the mid-1800s to the mid-1900s, the area was the location of a penitentiary, a sanatorium, and an asylum, as well as a quarry that reduced the height of the rocky hill. In 2003, when workers were excavating to prepare for a new highway, thousands of bodies of prisoners and patients from the sanatorium and asylum were discovered. It is estimated that up to 10,000 more people may be buried near Snake Hill, giving it a reputation for being one of the most haunted locations in New Jersey.

8. The Devil's Tower (Alpine)

This eerie structure was constructed in the early twentieth century for a sugar baron. The tower was connected to the baron's home through an underground tunnel. Legend says the baron's wife was once looking out from the tower when she saw her husband with another woman; the wife was so panicked that she jumped from the tower and died. In the decades since her death, tower visitors have reported a myriad of spooky occurrences, including noises, shadowy figures, and odd smells.

9. Clinton Road (West Milford)

10. Cranbury Inn (Cranbury)

New Mexico

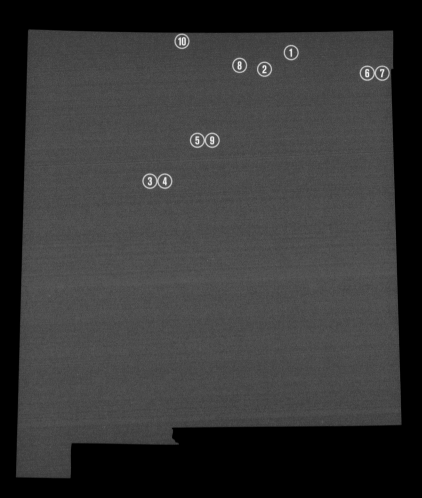

1. Dawson Cemetery (Dawson)

Dawson, New Mexico, is a ghost town in the county of Colfax, about a two-and-a-half-hour drive from Santa Fe, the nearest big city. A coal mining town in the early 1900s, Dawson reached a population of 9,000 people by around 1910. But tragedy struck in 1913 and again in 1923, when mine explosions killed a total of 386 men. By 1950, the mines were closed and the town was gone, save for the preserved cemetery. Now, in the still of night, some say the miners' helmet lights can be seen glowing in the cemetery.

2. James Hotel (Cimarron)

A Spanish Colonial building located in downtown Cimarron, the St. James Hotel was opened in 1872. Originally named the Lambert Inn in honor of its founder, Henry Lambert, the hotel's guest list was a who's who of lawmen and outlaws, hosting everyone from Wyatt Earp to Jesse James to Annie Oakley. The hotel quickly gained a reputation for violence, and 22 bullet holes are still visible in the dining room today. Restless spirits remain, as well, with many guests and staff reporting cold spots, pictures falling off walls, and the smell of cigar smoke.

3. Hotel Parq Central (Albuquerque)

In 1926, the Santa Fe Hospital opened in Albuquerque to treat employees of the Atchison, Topeka, and Santa Fe Railway. In the 1980s, the building was converted to a psychiatric facility and renamed Memorial Hospital. And in 2010, the former hospital was renovated into the Hotel Parq Central. Even before the hotel conversion, hospital patients and staff often complained about strange noises, voices, and even bedsheets being pulled from beds in the middle of the night. Now, ghost hunters book rooms in the hopes they'll catch a glimpse of a spirit or two.

4. (Above) KiMo Theater (Albuquerque)

The KiMo Theater in Albuquerque was built in 1927 by Oreste and Maria Bachechi, who commissioned the construction of the theater in honor of the Native Americans in the area. The theater opened to great fanfare, with legendary director Cecil B. DeMille sending a note of congratulations. Sadly, in 1951, a six-year-old boy was killed when a boiler exploded in the theater's basement. Now, patrons and performers say the boy's ghost is sometimes seen playing on a staircase, and theater staff leave doughnuts backstage for him. In the morning, the treats are often gone.

5. (Above) La Fonda on the Plaza (Santa Fe)

The history of this luxurious hotel dates back nearly 400 years; in fact, an inn was first opened on this site in the early seventeenth century. Numerous murders have taken place on the property, which is a probable explanation for the handful of ghosts that (locals claim) populate the hotel.

6. Hotel Eklund (Clayton)

This spooky hotel was built in the 1890s and included a gambling hall, saloon, and about two dozen guest rooms. Today, the hotel's Room 307 is supposedly haunted by the spirit of a former maid named Irene; visitors to this room have heard creaking floorboards and seen faces in the wallpaper.

7. Herzstein Museum (Clayton)

This museum features exhibits on the Dust Bowl and the Santa Fe Trail; it also contains artifacts from the early twentieth century. Ghost hunters say the building is home to multiple ghosts.

8. Elizabethtown

Located just off New Mexico State Road 38 is the ghost town of Elizabethtown. Founded in the late 1870s by Captain William H. Moore, who named the town after his daughter, Elizabeth, the gold mining town grew to a population of 7,000 by 1870 and was designated the first county seat of Colfax County. But within two years, the mines dried up, leaving only 100 residents. By 1917, the town was all but abandoned; but Elizabeth, the town's namesake, never left. She stayed in the town through thick and thin and is buried in the local cemetery.

9. La Posada Hotel (Santa Fe)

10. Foster's Hotel (Chama)

New York

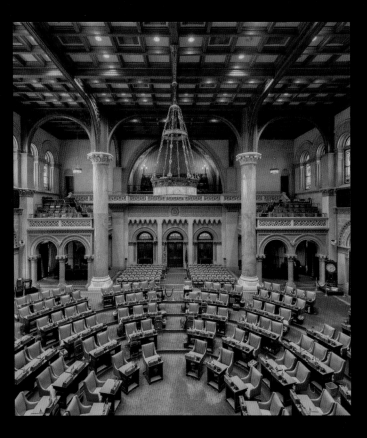

1. (Above and Right) State Capitol Building (Albany)

New York's state capitol building is a treasure trove of paranormal activity. A night watchman who died in the 1911 capitol fire supposedly still haunts the building's halls. Shadowy figures, flickering lights, and a hidden devil are known to spook both visitors and lawmakers.

2. (Left) United States Military Academy (West Point)

Could a major U.S. military college really be haunted? Apparently, yes. Since the mid-twentieth century, numerous reports have circulated about apparitions appearing in West Point's barracks in the middle of the night. Cadets have felt all kinds of mysterious presences; one cadet reported a sensation of someone sitting on his chest, and another saw an apparition appear out of a wall locker.

3. The Amityville House (Amityville)

In 1974, Ronald DeFeo Jr. murdered his entire family as they slept in their Long Island home in Amityville, New York. The murders became infamous not for the crime itself, but for the occurrences in the house after a new family moved in. The new owners, the Lutz family, moved out after only 28 days, claiming they'd seen green slime oozing from the walls, smelled horrible odors, and saw a creature with red eyes. One member of the family said he woke up at 3:15 a.m. every night—the exact time of the murders.

4. (Right) New Amsterdam Theatre (New York City)

Built between 1902 and 1903, the New Amsterdam Theater in New York City is one of the city's oldest surviving Broadway theaters. The theater opened with a production of Shakespeare's *A Midsummer Night's Dream*, and more recent shows have included *Mary Poppins* and *Aladdin*. But one performer, a *Ziegfeld Follies* chorus girl named Olive Thomas, has stuck around for every show. Thomas, who died by suicide in 1920, often appears to staff and patrons; she has been known to pat people on the shoulder and knock items off shelves.

New York

5. Palmyra Historical Museum (Palmyra)

Housed in a former nineteenth century hotel and tavern, the Palmyra Historical Museum features exhibits and memorabilia of local history. Twenty-three themed rooms teach visitors about the Erie Canal, Underground Railroad, Civil War, Women's Suffrage, and more. In addition to historical tours, ghost tours are popular at the site. Visitors frequently catch glowing orbs in photos and hear footsteps, whispers, and voices. Some also claim the house is home to several ghost cats who playfully run when chased, only to vanish!

6. (Below) Sleepy Hollow Cemetery
(Sleepy Hollow)

Sleepy Hollow's famous 90-acre cemetery is home to nearly 45,000 graves, including writer Washington Irving and other famous Northeast figures. Those who visit this eerie site will encounter plenty of elaborate monuments and gothic architecture.

7. (Left) Brooklyn Bridge (New York City)

One of the most instantly recognizable bridges in the world, the Brooklyn Bridge in New York city spans the East River, connecting the boroughs of Manhattan and Brooklyn. When it opened on May 24, 1883, it was the longest suspension bridge in the world. While it is an engineering marvel, more than 20 men lost their lives during its construction, and countless others have jumped from the bridge to die by suicide. Visitors to the bridge sometimes report hearing phantom screams, and some say the spirit of a headless worker chases taxis off the bridge.

8. (Right) Fort Ontario State Historic Site (Oswego)

Fort Ontario was originally created by the British in 1755 as a defense during the French and Indian War. The fort, situated on Lake Ontario, was attacked, destroyed, and rebuilt several times between its construction and the Civil War, and today it is part of the Fort Ontario State Historic Site Museum. With a long history of battles and violence, the fort is popular with ghost hunters. Many have seen apparitions, heard strange noises, and seen glowing orbs—even during the daylight hours.

9. Merchant's House Museum (New York City)

10. Wing's Castle (Millbrook)

is an empty patch of woods that features a strange, barren circle of dir
Known as the Devil's Tramping Ground, legend says that nothing can gro
in the circle of dirt, and animals refuse to cross its threshold. Rumo
also claims that any object left in the circle will be thrown out of
by morning, because, it is believed, the devil dances and paces
the circle at night, thinking of new ways to torment humanit

. (Above) The Biltmore Estate (Asheville)

overing 178,926 square feet of floor space, the Biltmore Estate is the largest privately-owned house in the
nited States. The mansion was built between 1889 and 1895 for George Washington Vanderbilt II; it is still
wned by members of the Vanderbilt family today. It is also open to the public for tours, and many visitors are
onvinced the huge estate is haunted. Guests have seen spirits roaming up and down staircases, heard the sounds
f laughter and clinking glasses in empty rooms; some visitors have even heard a voice calling for "George"

3. (Above) Omni Grove Park Inn (Asheville)

The Omni Grove Park Inn opened in 1913 at a site nestled in the Blue Ridge Mountains. The hotel h
hosted almost a dozen presidents, including William Howard Taft, Richard Nixon, and Barack Obam
But perhaps the hotel's most famous guest is the "Pink Lady," the inn's resident ghost. Believed
be the spirit of a woman who fell to her death from the fifth floor of the hotel in 1920, the ghost oft
appears as a pink mist. Some guests have even seen the apparition of a woman in a pink ball gow

6. The Country Squire (Kenansville)

The ghost of Joe West, this restaurant's original owner, is rumored to haunt the property. Random footsteps, noises, and even a dartboard's flying darts are all known to greet diners.

4. (Above) Cape Hatteras Lighthouse (Buxton)

Cape Hatteras Lighthouse stands on Hatteras Island in the Outer Banks. Before the lighthouse's construction, the area was known for shipwrecks, giving it the nickname "Graveyard of the Atlantic." The original lighthouse was lit in 1803, with a newer tower constructed in 1870. Visitors can climb 257 steps to reach the top of the tower and keep an eye out for the ghostly figure of man who is sometimes seen wandering the beach. Others have seen a black and white cat in the lighthouse, which disappears if someone gets close.

5. Lydia's Bridge (Jamestown)

In Jamestown, North Carolina, a graffiti-covered concrete overpass marks the location of Lydia's Bridge. Since the 1920s, motorists passing by have often told a story of a woman in a white gown who flags down drivers and asks for a ride. But the Good Samaritans who drive her home discover she has disappeared when they arrive at her address. And the legend has a ring of truth to it: in 1920, a 30-year-old woman was killed at the bridge in a car accident. Shortly after that tragic event, tales of the vanishing hitchhiker began.

7. (Above) The Carolina Inn (Chapel Hill)

This 1920s inn is reportedly haunted by a doctor who lived in the inn during the middle twentieth century. His spirit is known to lock guest doors, including his former Room 256. This inn is also known for unusual smells, random piano music, and curtains that randomly open and close.

8. Brown Mountain Lights (Linville)

Patterns of unusual lights have appeared at night above the Brown Mountain for hundreds of years. The lights change shape, color, and size. Universities, as well as the U.S. government, have investigated the lights; however, no legitimate explanation of their origin has been found.

9. Grand Old Lady Hotel (Balsam)

10. The Duke Mansion (Charlotte)

North Dakota

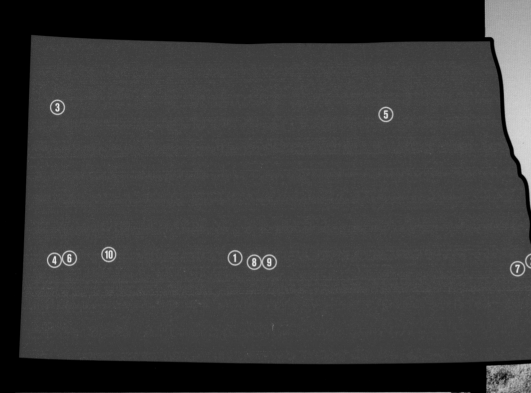

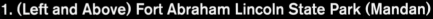

1. (Left and Above) Fort Abraham Lincoln State Park (Mandan)
Established in 1907, Fort Abraham Lincoln State Park, located just south of Mandan, is the oldest state park in North Dakota. Standing on the site of a former cavalry post, the park features artifacts and reconstructions of Native American villages and U.S. military buildings, including a replica of Lieutenant Colonel George A. Custer's house. Some say that Custer and his wife, Libby, haunt the house, occasionally peering at visitors through windows. Guests have also heard footsteps, whispering, and crying in several other buildings throughout the park.

2. The Children's Museum at Yunker Farm (Fargo)
The spirit of Sarah Yunker, the wife of this farm's former owner, is known to haunt this Fargo property.

3. Old Armory (Williston)
This century-old building is listed in the National Register of Historic Places. Legend says mannequins inside the armory move around on their own accord. Armory visitors have also heard unusual voices and spooky whispers.

4. (Above) Chateau De Mores (Medora)

Built by the Marquis de Mores, a native of France and a frontier ranchman in the Badlands of the Dakota Territory, the Chateau de Mores is now a State Historic Site. The Marquis, who ran a cattle operation, lived in the house with his family from 1883 to 1886, until his business failed. In 1936, the home was gifted to the state and was opened to the public for tours. Strange occurrences are often reported at the site, including shadowy figures, lights that come on in the empty home, and cold spots throughout the chateau.

5. Totten Trail Historic Inn (Fort Totten)

The Totten Trail Inn is located within the Fort Totten State Historic Site. The fort was established in 1867 to help keep the peace between two Native American tribes, and it was later used as a Native American boarding school. The building that now houses the inn was used for employee housing until the school shut down in 1960. According to rumor, a man and woman who died in the building still haunt the inn today. Guests claim that they are sometimes followed throughout the hotel by shadowy figures.

6. Medora Fudge & Ice Cream Depot (Medora)

The spirit of a mysterious woman haunts Medora's popular ice cream shop; she only appears on her birthday

7. Riverside Cemetery (Fargo)

Fargo's Riverside Cemetery occupies a stretch of quiet green parkland next to the Red River. While it may seem like a quiet place to rest in peace, the cemetery is known for the strange audio sounds that can be picked up with recording equipment. Rumor says that a certain mausoleum in the graveyard is particularly noisy, and if a recording device is placed next to it, it will record the sound of knocking coming from within the cold stone structure.

8. Former Governor's Mansion (Bismarck)

The current North Dakota Governor's Residence in Bismarck is actually the third residence to house the state's governors. A 1960s-era residence was demolished in 2018, but the original governor's mansion, built in 1884, is now a museum run by the State Historical Society of North Dakota. The mansion was the home of 20 of North Dakota's governors, including Frank Briggs, who died of tuberculosis in the master bedroom of the mansion in 1898. Many believe he still haunts the house; visitors have heard footsteps and seen the bedroom door open and close on its own.

9. Liberty Memorial Building (Bismarck)

10. St. Joseph's Hospital (Dickinson)

Ohio

1. (Above and Below) Ohio State Reformatory (Mansfield)

The Ohio State Reformatory was made famous when it was used as the location for the prison in the 1994 film *The Shawshank Redemption*. The prison was built between 1886 and 1910 and was in use until 1990, and is now open to the public for tours. At least 215 inmates died in the prison and are now buried in a cemetery next door. Tour guides often report hearing voices and footsteps in the cold hallways of the reformatory, perhaps of prisoners who never left their confinement.

2. (Above) Moonville Tunnel (McArthur)

In 1870, Moonville, Ohio, was a small mining town of 100 residents in what is now McArthur. One of the few remnants of the tiny town, which consisted of only a few buildings, is the Moonville Tunnel, a concrete expanse that covered an old railway. Legend says the only way out of the town was to walk along the train tracks through the tunnel, and numerous people died on the tracks. Now, visitors to the area say that after dark, the figure of a man with a lantern can be seen wandering through the tunnel.

3. Franklin Castle (Ohio City)

Located in historic Ohio City, one of the oldest neighborhoods in Cleveland, Ohio, Franklin Castle is also known as the Tiedemann House. The house was built between 1881 and 1883 for German immigrant Hannes Tiedemann and his family. Sadly, four of Tiedemann's children died in the house in the late 1800s, fueling suspicion of foul play. Today, the castle is privately owned, but it doesn't stop the rumor that Franklin Castle is the most haunted house in Ohio. Owners have claimed to see ghostly figures and to hear crying in almost every area of the house.

Ohio

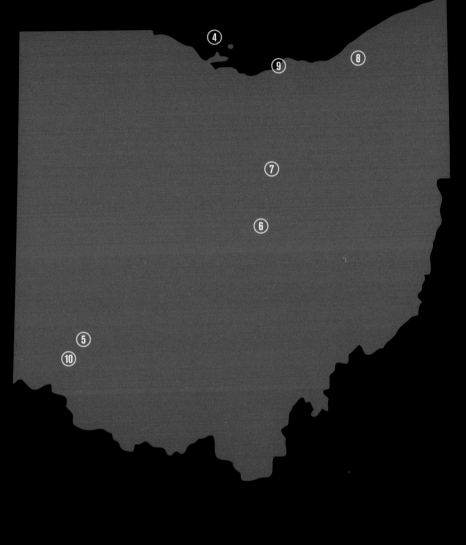

5. (Below) The Golden Lamb (Lebanon)

This popular restaurant and inn is Ohio's oldest; it first opened in 1803. In fact, multiple U.S. presidents have dined inside its famous walls.. In addition to its scrumptious food, the Golden Lamb serves up its own share of the paranormal. One ghost—the spirit of a woman named Sarah Stubbs—supposedly wanders the building. Another ghost is the spirit of Clement L. Vallandigham, a politician who accidentally killed himself inside the inn. Fortunately, all of the inn's spirits are said to be welcoming.

4. South Bass Island Lighthouse (Put-in-Bay)

Owned by Ohio State University, this creepy lighthouse has a dark history. The lighthouse's first keeper, Harry Riley, died in a state hospital in 1899 after going insane. One year earlier, an island visitor named Harry Anderson died by suicide when he jumped into Lake Erie from an island dock. Today, lighthouse visitors report hearing unusual noises, random footsteps, and doors slamming.

6. The Buxton Inn (Granville)

This 200-year-old hotel is one of Ohio's grandest establishments. It's also home to multiple ghosts, including the spirits of an opera star and Major Buxton, a former owner's cat. Numerous hotel patrons have also seen orbs appearing in photos that were taken at the inn.

7. (Above) Malabar Farm State Park (Lucas)

Malabar Farm near Lucas, Ohio, was founded in 1939 by Pulitzer Prize-winning author and conservationist Louis Bromfield. Bromfield's experimental farm attracted both environmentalists and celebrities, and in 1945, the farm was the venue for the wedding of Humphrey Bogart and Lauren Bacall. But in 1896, long before Bromfield purchased the farm, a teenaged girl named Ceely Rose poisoned her family in a house on the property. The entire farm is now a state park, and visitors believe the Ceely Rose House, where the murders occurred, is haunted by the young killerf.

8. Punderson Manor (Newbury)

Northeast Ohio's Punderson State Park is about 30 minutes from downtown Cleveland. In 1929, the land encompassing the park was bought by Detroit millionaire Karl Long, who began building a mansion on the property. But when Long lost his fortune during the Great Depression, construction stalled; the property was later sold to the state, which turned the building into a resort now known as the Punderson Manor State Park Lodge. Rumors of hauntings began in the 1970s and continue today, with staff and guests reporting sounds from empty rooms, cold spots, items moving, and ghostly apparitions.

9. Lorain Palace Theater (Lorain)

10. (Right) Kings Island Amusement Park (Mason)

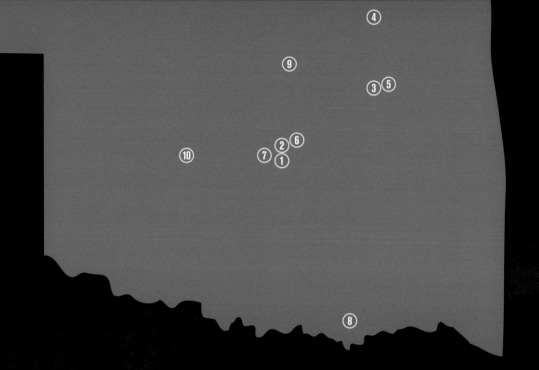

1. The Skirvin Hilton Hotel (Oklahoma City)

The oldest hotel in Oklahoma City, the Skirvin Hilton Hotel opened in 1911 and is listed in the National Register of Historic Places. The hotel spans three 14-floor towers, which were constructed in an Art Deco architectural style. Legend says that the original owner of the hotel, W.B. Skirvin, had an affair with a maid, who later killed herself and their illegitimate child by throwing herself from a tenth floor window. Staff and guests frequently complain of noises, slamming doors, and moving objects, especially on the tenth floor.

2. Stone Lion Inn (Guthrie)

Guthrie's famous bed and breakfast was once a funeral parlor. The business's history with the dead could explain why visitors have reported paranormal experiences over the years.

3. Gilcrease Museum (Tulsa)

The Gilcrease Museum features the world's largest collection of art from the American West. The museum is named after Thomas Gilcrease, an art collector, oil man, and philanthropist who gave his collection to the city of Tulsa in 1958. Gilcrease died in 1962 and was interred in a mausoleum on the grounds of the museum. Vsitors and staff believe that he loved his art so much that his ghost now wanders the halls of the museum. Night guards often hear loud noises, slamming doors, and feel cold breezes.

4. Gravity Hill (Bartlesville)

Legend says that a car placed in neutral at the bottom of this hill will roll backwards . . . uphill.

5. Cain's Ballroom (Tulsa)

Built in 1924, acclaimed live music venue Cain's Ballroom was originally used as an automobile garage. By the early 1940s, the entertainment space was gaining popularity for featuring "western swing" music, earning the nickname "the Carnegie Hall of Western Swing." While the ballroom is one of the most popular music clubs in the world, it's also known for its ghost stories. Some say that the spirits of many who performed at the venue still linger at the site, and visitors have reported cold spots, glowing orbs, phantom singing, and lights turning on and off.

6. The Dominion House (Guthrie)

The Dominion House in Guthrie is an events center, hotel, and restaurant popular for weddings and parties. But when it was built in 1923, it was the Masonic Children's Home and was one of the largest children's facilities in the state. Hundreds of children were given shelter in the home until it closed in 1978. The building was abandoned for several decades, during which time passersby reported seeing ghostly faces peering from windows. Even today, visitors often see apparitions and dark shadows, and hear the sounds of crying and footsteps.

7. Historic Fort Reno (El Reno)

This former military camp was established in 1874. Visitors to the camp have reported random footsteps, doors that mysteriously open and close, and cold spots.

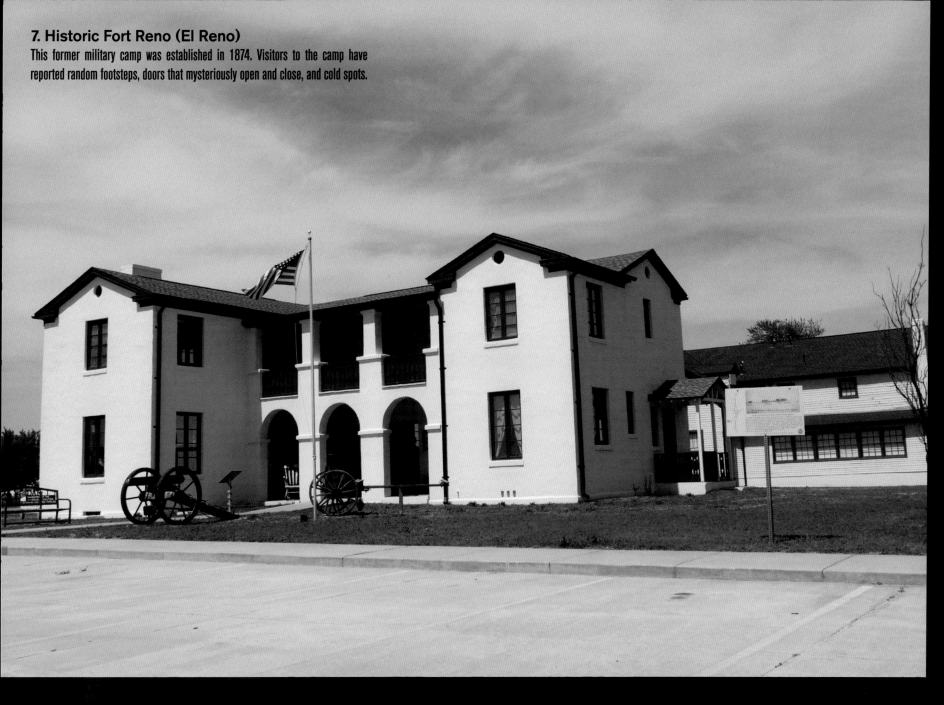

8. Fort Washita Historic Site & Museum (Durant)

Located in Durant, the Fort Washita Historic Site is a former United States military post. The post was established in 1842 by General (and later President) Zachary Taylor, as a way to keep the peace between Native American tribes in the area. The site was abandoned after the Civil War, but it was later restored by the Oklahoma Historical Society in 1962. The fort is said to be haunted by a ghost nicknamed "Aunt Jane," a headless apparition who wanders the area. Visitors have also heard drums, the sound of a bugle, and footsteps.

9. Cherokee Strip Museum (Perry)

10. Dead Women Crossing (Weatherford)

Oregon

3. (Above and Below) Heceta Head Lighthouse Keeper's Home (Florence)

Located on the Oregon coast 13 miles north of Florence, the Heceta Head Lighthouse shines a beacon that is visible up to 21 nautical miles away. The light was first lit in 1894 and automated in 1963. The home that once sheltered the lighthouse keepers and their families is now a bed and breakfast. According to rumor, the son of a keeper drowned many decades ago, and the keeper's wife now haunts the home, searching for her child. Staff and guests have seen indentations on freshly made beds, heard footsteps and seen objects fly off of shelves.

1. The Shanghai Tunnels (Portland)

The Shanghai Tunnels, also known as the Old Portland Underground, are a group of passages running underneath the Old Town Chinatown neighborhood of Portland. The tunnels, which have existed since at least the nineteenth century, were built to connect basements of hotels and taverns on the Willamette River, allowing merchants to deliver goods underground. But some stories tell of gangsters and criminals using the tunnels for nefarious purposes, too. Now, many believe the tunnels are haunted; visitors report hearing voices and feeling hands tug at clothing.

2. Lafayette Pioneer Cemetery (Dayton)

Oregon's Willamette Valley is home to 70 percent of the state's population and is especially well-known for its wine industry. But those who are more interested in a good scare can head to the Lafayette Pioneer Cemetery in Dayton. Legend says the graveyard is haunted by the ghost of a woman named Anna Marple; Maple's son was hanged for murdering a shop owner. Witnesses to the execution claimed Marple cursed the town, and now cemetery visitors report hearing laughter and seeing the apparition of a woman wandering the grounds.

5. Wolf Creek Inn (Wolf Creek)

Stagecoach pioneers erected this historic inn at the end of the nineteenth century; writer Jack London even once stayed the night. Hotel patrons have experienced all kinds of paranormal spookiness, including slamming doors, piano music, and chairs that randomly move.

6. Bush House Museum (Salem)

Salem's 1870s-era mansion is home to a spirit named Eugenia; she is the daughter of Asahel Bush II, the home's original owner. Her spirit supposedly randomly turns the mansion's air conditioning system on and off.

7. (Left) Benson Hotel (Portland)

This landmark Portland hotel was built by Norwegian immigrant Simon Benson in 1913. Hotel guests today claim to see his spirit wandering around the elegant building. Other spirits supposedly lurk around the hotel's hallways and lobby, too.

8. Highway 101 Bandage Man (Cannon Beach)

In the 1950s, spooky stories began popping up in Cannon Beach, Oregon, a town that sits on the coast of the Pacific. According to the tales, the ghost of a man, bloodied and covered in bandages, often haunts the roads and forests of Cannon Beach, sometimes knocking on the windows of teenagers as they make out in parked cars. Legend says he was a logger, injured in a terrible accident. As an ambulance sped him away, it was caught in a landslide; when rescuers reached the vehicle, the bandaged man was gone.

4. (Above) Pittock Mansion (Portland)

A French Renaissance-style chateau located in Portland, the Pittock Mansion was originally built as a private home for newspaper editor Henry Pittock. The 46-room mansion, which was finished in 1914, was a state-of-the-art marvel, complete with an elevator, intercoms, and a central vacuum system. Pittock and his wife both died soon after the home was finished, never able to fully enjoy its luxury. Today, the mansion is open for tours, and many visitors are convinced that the Pittocks never left. Guests have witnessed windows open and close, heard footsteps, and seen apparitions of the couple.

9. Hot Lake Hotel (Hot Lake)

10. Eugene Masonic Cemetery (Eugene)

Pennsylvania

1. (Above and Right) Eastern State Penitentiary (Philadelphia)

With its unique "wagon wheel" design and emphasis on reform over punishment, the Eastern State Penitentiary in Philadelphia was considered the world's first true penitentiary when it opened in 1829. The prison housed inmates until 1971, including Al Capone; today, it is a museum and historic site. It is also considered one of the most haunted places in America, with reports of hauntings occurring as far back as 1940. Guards, inmates, and visitors have all claimed to have heard voices and laughter and seen dark shadows and ghostly faces within the cells.

2. (Above) Gettysburg Battlefield

One of the most famous battles of the Civil War, the Battle of Gettysburg occurred from July 1 to July 3, 1863; the battle is often considered the war's turning point. Approximately 50,000 soldiers lost their lives on the southern Pennsylvania battlefield. Today, the Gettysburg National Military Park welcomes three million visitors a year, including plenty of ghost hunters. With its violent history, it's no wonder that visitors have seen apparitions of soldiers, heard shouts of military commands, and even smelled the scent of blood.

3. Hill View Manor (New Castle)

Originally known as the Lawrence County Home for the Aged, Hill View Manor opened in New Castle in 1926; it housed the mentally ill, destitute, and elderly. In 1944, the home was accused of mismanagement, and it underwent decades of restructuring until it became a dedicated skilled nursing center. The manor was closed and abandoned in 2004. Many believe there are residents who never left, and visitors have heard footsteps, voices, and slamming doors.

4. Jean Bonnet Tavern (Bedford)

Bedford's famous tavern opened in 1762; in fact, George Washington's troops apparently slept at the tavern during a march. For decades, tavern guests have reported taps on the shoulders, unusual noises, and ghostly figures dining in the restaurant.

Pennsylvania

5. (Below) Mishler's Theatre (Altoona)

The Mishler Theater in Altoona, Pennsylvania, was built by local theater manager Isaac Charles Mishler in 1906. After Mishler retired and sold the theater, it suffered from neglect for several decades. The Blair County Arts Foundation restored the building in 1969; the inaugural show performed on the renovated stage was *The Sound of Music*. Many believe that Mishler now haunts his theater, with patrons often smelling cigar smoke and seeing a figure dressed in early 1900s clothing loitering near his old office.

6. (Right) Hotel Bethlehem (Bethlehem)

The Historic Hotel Bethlehem in Bethlehem tands on the site of the city's first house, which was built in 1741 by members of the Moravian Brethren. In 1823, the Moravians constructed a hotel, known as the Eagle Hotel, on the property, and in 1921, the Eagle Hotel became the Hotel Bethlehem. With its long history, it's not surprising that guests insist the hotel is haunted. Ghostly apparitions in old-fashioned clothing are sometimes seen throughout the hotel, and Room 932 is known for its glowing orbs, flashing lights, and mysterious color-changing wallpaper.

7. (Left) Cathedral of Learning (Pittsburgh)

The University of Pittsburgh's famous 42-story skyscraper is supposedly haunted by the ghost of Mary Schenley, a major philanthropist. Schenley donated the majority of her estate to the city of Pittsburgh before her death in 1903. Her spirit has been seen roaming the building's ballroom at night.

8. Coulterville Cemetery (McKeesport)

This sprawling cemetery was built on the site of a former orphanage. Legend says that a fire one nineteenth century evening claimed the lives of all of the orphanage's children. For years, cemetery visitors have heard the cries of children; some visitors have even seen smoke in the air. After leaving the burial ground, other visitors have reported child-size handprints on their car windows!

9. Farnsworth House Inn (Gettysburg)

10. Hansell Road (Buckingham)

Rhode Island

2. (Above) White Horse Tavern (Newport)
Considered the oldest operating restaurant in the United States, the White Horse Tavern in Newport has been serving patrons since 1673. The building that houses the restaurant is even older, having been constructed in 1652 as a private home. The tavern is not only the oldest restaurant in America, but also, according to some, the most haunted. Diners tell stories of seeing figures in Colonial-period dress and of hearing a child crying when no one is around. Staff at the tavern often hear footsteps on the upper floor when they're closing up for the night.

1. The Conjuring Farmhouse (Burrillville)
The Farm on Round Top Road in Burrillville is better known as "The Conjuring House," made famous by the 2013 film *The Conjuring.* According to the Perron family, who bought the eighteenth century farmhouse in the 1970s, the house was plagued with sinister paranormal activity. Spirits in the house attacked them, lifted their beds, and stopped clocks at exactly 3:07 a.m. The family moved out in 1980, and today, the home is owned by ghost hunters who welcome the public for tours of the eerie property.

3. Fort Wetherill (Jamestown)
A former artillery fort on Conanicut Island in Jamestown, Fort Wetherill was built in 1895 on the site of an existing Revolutionary War-era fort. The fort was in use until World War II, after which it was abandoned. But in 1972, the fort was acquired by the state, which created the 61.5-acre Fort Wetherill State Park. Since its earliest days, stories have been told of a phantom dog that haunts the fort. The black dog can be heard growling, barking, and howling, and some visitors have seen it staring at them before disappearing into a wall.

4. (Above and Left) Belcourt Castle (Newport)

Newport's Belcourt Castle was built to be a summer cottage for socialite and U.S. Representative Oliver Belmont. The 50,000-square-foot, 60-room villa featured an entire first floor dedicated to carriage space and stables for Belmont's prized horses. The home is now open for tours and as an event space, and has welcomed its fair share of ghost hunters. Many have seen a figure in monk robes wandering the grounds, and some say screams and moans emanate from the ballroom.

Rhode Island

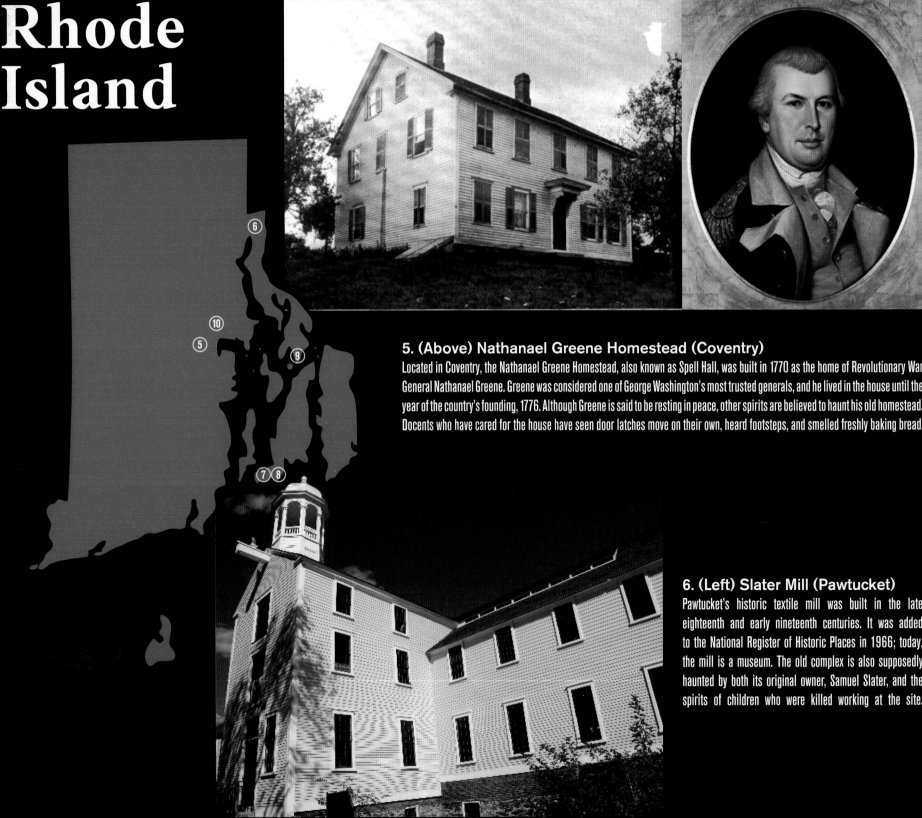

5. (Above) Nathanael Greene Homestead (Coventry)

Located in Coventry, the Nathanael Greene Homestead, also known as Spell Hall, was built in 1770 as the home of Revolutionary War General Nathanael Greene. Greene was considered one of George Washington's most trusted generals, and he lived in the house until the year of the country's founding, 1776. Although Greene is said to be resting in peace, other spirits are believed to haunt his old homestead. Docents who have cared for the house have seen door latches move on their own, heard footsteps, and smelled freshly baking bread.

6. (Left) Slater Mill (Pawtucket)

Pawtucket's historic textile mill was built in the late eighteenth and early nineteenth centuries. It was added to the National Register of Historic Places in 1966; today, the mill is a museum. The old complex is also supposedly haunted by both its original owner, Samuel Slater, and the spirits of children who were killed working at the site.

7. (Above and Below) The Breakers (Newport)

Cornelius Vanderbilt II's massive Gilded Age mansion is more than 125,000 square feet in size. This historical landmark features 70 rooms, 30-foot-tall walkway gates, opulent gardens, and countless brilliant details. The mansion is also, legend says, where the spirit of Cornelius's wife Alice is said to roam.

8. (Above) Seaview Terrace (Newport)

This sprawling, 40,000-square-foot mansion was erected in the early twentieth century by Edson Bradley, a wealthy liquor businessman. For years, the property has been marked by a series of unusual occurrences, including disembodied voices, dark shadows, and possible spirits. One of the ghosts is reportedly the spirit of Mrs. Bradley, Edson's wife.

9. Colt State Park (Bristol)

10. Saint Mary's Church (West Warwick)

South Carolina

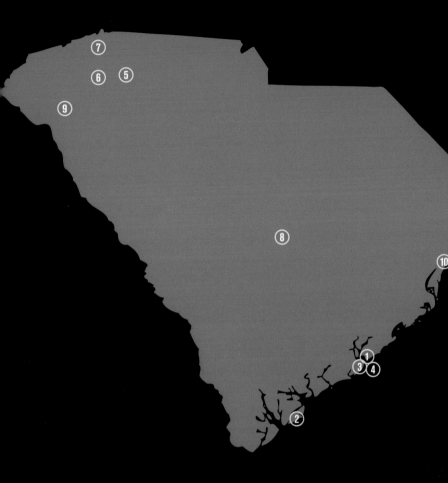

2. (Above and Below) Stoney Baynard Ruins (Hilton Head Island)

The Stoney-Baynard Plantation, also called the Baynard Ruins, is located on Hilton Head Island in South Carolina. Dating back to the late 1700s, the plantation was built by Revolutionary War hero Captain Jack Stoney, and in 1837 became the property of William Baynard. Much of the plantation was burned down in the late 1800s, but the foundations, made of a mix of oyster shells, lime, sand and water, remain. Some say Baynard remains as well, with many visitors claiming to have seen his spirit wandering the property, sometimes followed by a ghostly funeral procession.

. Battery Carriage House Inn (Charleston)

he Battery Carriage Inn in Charleston was originally built as a private home in the 1800s. The home survived e 1863 Siege of Charleston during the Civil War and was later purchased by a Union army colonel. In the 980s, the historic house was converted into a boutique hotel, but tourists are not the only guests at this inn. everal rooms are home to resident ghosts, including Room 8, which is famous for the ghostly apparition of a eadless torso, and Room 10, which is home to a friendly ghost who shares the bed with the room's occupant.

3. (Above) Old Charleston Jail (Charleston)

Constructed in 1802, the Old Charleston Jail in Charleston once housed both Civil War prisoners of war, and Charleston's most notorious criminals, including some of the last nineteenth century high-seas pirates. Today, it is one of 1,400 historic buildings within Charleston's Old and Historic District, and is open for tours, including nighttime ghost tours. The jail is haunted by many former inmates, and staff and visitors have heard voices and slamming doors, found ghostly faces in their photos, and seen footprints in deserted areas of the jail.

4. Dock Street Theatre (Charleston)

This exquisitely-preserved historic theater first opened in 1736. Its popularity waned during the Reconstruction era, and it suffered significant damage during the city's 1886 earthquake. Fortunately, it returned to its glorious self in the twentieth century. Today, two ghosts reportedly haunt the building's premises, including the spirit of John Wilkes Booth's father, Junius Booth!

5. Seven Devils Bridge (Woodruff)

Woodruff's Seven Devils Bridge looks like an unassuming stretch of road, but locals tell frightening tales of the location. According to legend, seven slaves were hanged from the bridge long ago, and today their angry spirits roam the area. Every night at midnight, the ghosts are especially active, forbidding anyone from crossing the bridge. Green, glowing lights can be seen in the distance, and those who attempt to cross the bridge at midnight are said to be driven mad by the spirits of the slaves.

6. Gassaway Mansion (Greenville)

The Gassaway Mansion, also known as Isaqueena, is a 40-room estate located in Greenville. The home was built between 1919 and 1924 by banker and textile mill owner Walter Gassaway; the mansion was designed by his wife, Minnie. The house has been used as an apartment building, an art school, and a church, and is now an event space. Walter died in 1930, but he loved the mansion so much that he is said to still haunt the eclectic home.

7. (Above) Poinsett Bridge (Greenville County)

Believed to be South Carolina's oldest bridge, this 130-foot structure was built more than 200 years ago and remains largely intact. It was once part of a road from Columbia to the Saluda Mountains. In recent years, bridge visitors have encountered all kinds of eerie activity, including orbs and shadowy figures.

8. (Above) Elmwood Cemetery (Columbia)

Columbia's famous cemetery is home to more than 25,000 graves across its 125 acres.

9. Crybaby Bridge (Anderson)

10. The Hermitage (Murrells Inlet)

South Dakota

①
②
③
④

1. Sica Hollow State Park (Sisseton)

Named for the Dakota word for "bad" or "evil," Sica (pronounced SHE-chah) Hollow State Park in Sisseton is the source of many scary legends. The streams and bogs in the park gurgle with reddish water, which Native Americans believed to be the blood of their ancestors, and the cause of supernatural occurrences in the area. Settlers began disappearing in the mid-nineteenth century, with some blaming a "Bigfoot"-type creature. Today, those who are brave enough to camp in the park hear voices and chanting and see apparitions of Native American braves.

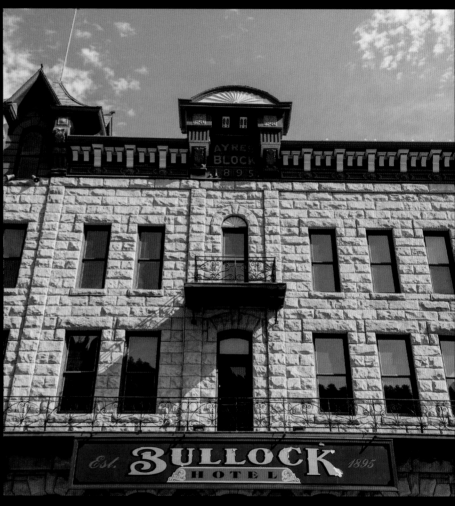

2. (Left and Above) Historic Bullock Hotel (Deadwood)

Located in downtown Deadwood, the Historic Bullock Hotel is named after the town's first sheriff, Seth Bullock. Bullock lived in Deadwood from 1876 until his death in 1919, and he built the hotel, the first in the town, in 1894. Today, the hotel is much the same as it was during Bullock's time, and many believe the sheriff still oversees his hotel. Staff and guests have noticed items moving on their own, showers that turn on and off by themselves, and the feeling of a presence on the second and third floors.

3. (Above) Historic Adams House (Deadwood)

This Victorian Deadwood home was once described as "the grandest house west of the Mississippi." Built in 1892 by Harris and Anna Franklin, this home was later purchased by W.E. Adams. Adams died of a stroke in 1934, and following his death, his wife reportedly claimed her deceased husband's spirit could be heard walking around on the second floor. Today, the house is a museum.

4. Homestake Opera House (Lead)

Lead's Historic Homestake Opera House was originally both a theater and a recreation center. The building was constructed in 1914 and included a 1,000-seat auditorium, pool, bowling alley, and library. But in 1984, a fire destroyed much of the building, and it sat abandoned until the city began a restoration project in 1995, which has slowly and meticulously brought the opera house back to life. Patrons admiring the historic building have also reported hearing phantom voices and seeing shadowy figures creeping through hallways.

South Dakota

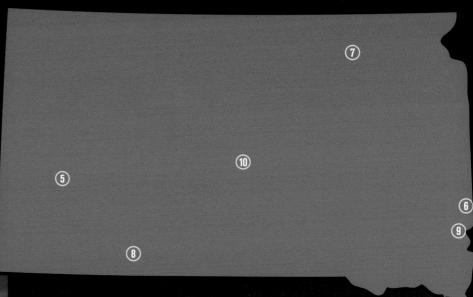

5. (Below) Hotel Alex Johnson (Rapid City)

Alex Carlton Johnson, a railroad businessman, opened his Rapid City hotel in 1928. For decades, the site hosted an impressive slate of celebrities, presidents, and other prominent figures. Unfortunately, the hotel has also been home to multiple deaths, including a wedding bride and Johnson himself. Guests have observed ghosts, unusual sounds, and mysterious shadows during stays at the hotel.

6. (Right) Devil's Gulch (Garretson)

In September 1876, famous outlaw Jesse James was running from the law. He had attempted to rob a bank in Minnesota and then spent weeks fleeing west on horseback. After passing through the town of Garretson, Jesse's horse came to a ravine, now known as Devil's Gulch. Instead of searching for a way around, Jesse spurred his horse on and jumped the chasm, escaping his stunned pursuers. Jesse may have been lucky, but visitors say the gulch is home to many spirits, and perhaps even the Devil himself, who is said to wander the grounds at night.

7. Easton Castle (Aberdeen)

Built in 1888, this Victorian home is reportedly haunted by Leslie Gage, the niece of the author L. Frank Baum. Gage, rumor says, was the inspiration for Dorothy in *The Wizard of Oz.*

8. (Left and Above) Wounded Knee (Pine Ridge Indian Reservation)

The town of Wounded Knee lies within the Pine Ridge Indian Reservation. The area is said to be the location where the bones and heart of Lakota war leader Crazy Horse were buried by his family. But the town's most famous for the tragic Wounded Knee Massacre of 1890, when the U.S. 7th Cavalry Regiment killed 300 Lakota men, women, and children. Many of the dead were unceremoniously buried in a mass grave, which was later marked by a monument. Visitors often hear the sobs and cries of women and children carried by the wind.

9. Orpheum Theater (Sioux Falls)

10. LaFramboise Island Nature Area (Pierre)

Tennessee

1. (Left and Above) Roaring Fork Motor Trail (Gatlinburg)
This 5.5-mile trail in Great Smoky Mountains National Park is supposedly haunted by a ghost named Lucy. She was once a young girl who died when her family's cabin was destroyed by a fire in the early twentieth century. Travelers along the trail periodically spot the barefoot ghost wandering along the road.

2. (Above) Tennessee State Prison (Nashville)

This maximum security facility housed violent criminals throughout the nineteenth and twentieth centuries. It was notorious for its treatment of inmates, who were forced to work under brutal conditions. The prison closed in 1992; since its closure, visitors have reporterd all kinds of creepy activity, including screams and footsteps.

3. The Bell Witch Cave (Adams)

Located in Adams, the Bell Witch Cave sits on property once owned by farmer John Bell Sr. and his family. According to local legend, the Bell family was haunted by an entity from 1817 until 1821. Dubbed the Bell Witch, the ghost was said to shapeshift, first appearing as a black dog, and often spoke out loud to the family. After the Bell family left the area, the witch moved to the cave, where numerous brave explorers have reported flashlights failing, thumping noises, and screams coming from deep within the underground chamber.

4. McKamey Manor (Summertown)

Spirits and ghosts may scare us now and then, but for the most part, they leave us with nothing more than a sense of mystery and curiosity. But McKamey Manor in Summertown, Tennessee, which bills itself as a "survival horror" house, provides very real—and sometimes very dangerous—terror. Founded by Russ McKamey, the "haunted house" provides tours that last up to eight hours, subjecting visitors to very real psychological and even physical torture. Participants must sign a waiver before attempting to complete the entire tour, which no one has ever done.

5. Sensabaugh Tunnel (Church Hill)

The Sensabaugh Tunnel near Church Hill was built in the 1920s by Edward Sensabaugh, who, according to local legend, killed his family and dumped their bodies into the creek nearby. Now, the tunnel is considered one of the most haunted tunnels in the world, with visitors reporting the sounds of screams, crying babies, and gunshots. Some say that if you turn your car engine off in the middle of the tunnel, the car won't restart until the ghost of Edward appears in your rearview mirror.

Tennessee

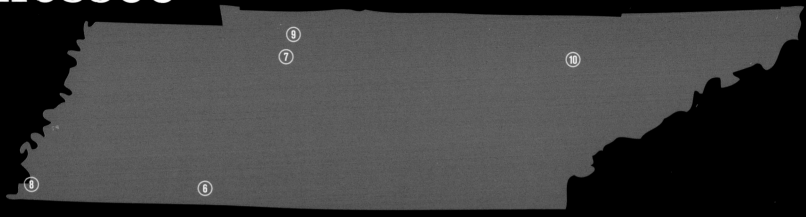

6. (Above and Right) Shiloh National Military Park (Hardin County)

Commemorating the Civil War Battle of Shiloh, Shiloh National Military Park spans almost 4,000 acres in Hardin County. The battle occurred on April 6 and 7, 1862, and resulted in approximately 24,000 soldiers killed, wounded, or missing. The northeast corner of the park contains a cemetery, where thousands of mostly Union soldiers were buried. The park is believed to be haunted by many of these soldiers, with visitors seeing apparitions and hearing voices. Some also say a pond in the park occasionally turns red, a reminder of the blood that was spilled.

8. (Above) Orpheum Theater (Memphis)

This famous Memphis theater opened its doors in 1928, and over the years, it's had multiple renovations. It's also where Mary the ghost is known to greet patrons and even watch theater performances.

7. (Above and Below) Carnton Historic Home (Franklin)

On November 30, 1864, the Civil War Battle of Franklin was fought in Franklin. Occurring less than a mile from Carnton, a home owned by John and Carrie McGavock, more than 1,750 Confederate soldiers lost their lives in the battle. Carnton, a sprawling, two-story mansion, became a makeshift field hospital. Three hundred soldiers were given shelter in Carnton, with hundreds more on the surrounding property. Inevitably, many lost their lives; those who tour the mansion today say the soldiers never left. Their spirits are often seen roaming the property, especially during the autumn months.

9. (Above) Tennessee State Capitol (Nashville)

10. The Drummond Bridge (Briceville)

Texas

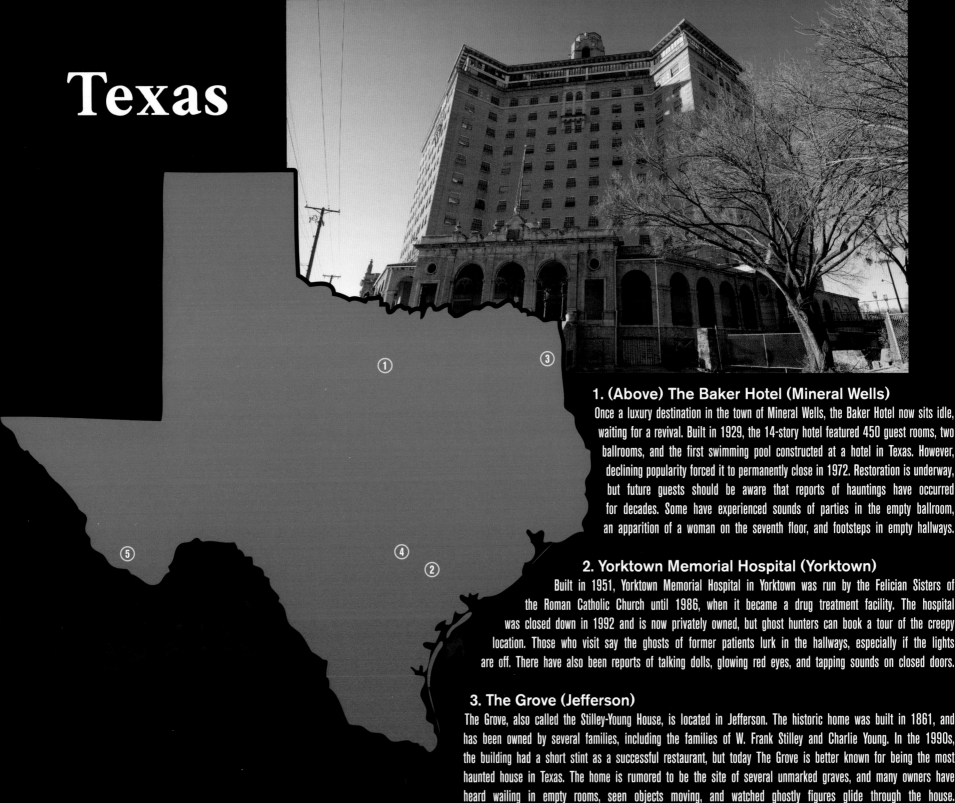

1. (Above) The Baker Hotel (Mineral Wells)

Once a luxury destination in the town of Mineral Wells, the Baker Hotel now sits idle, waiting for a revival. Built in 1929, the 14-story hotel featured 450 guest rooms, two ballrooms, and the first swimming pool constructed at a hotel in Texas. However, declining popularity forced it to permanently close in 1972. Restoration is underway, but future guests should be aware that reports of hauntings have occurred for decades. Some have experienced sounds of parties in the empty ballroom, an apparition of a woman on the seventh floor, and footsteps in empty hallways.

2. Yorktown Memorial Hospital (Yorktown)

Built in 1951, Yorktown Memorial Hospital in Yorktown was run by the Felician Sisters of the Roman Catholic Church until 1986, when it became a drug treatment facility. The hospital was closed down in 1992 and is now privately owned, but ghost hunters can book a tour of the creepy location. Those who visit say the ghosts of former patients lurk in the hallways, especially if the lights are off. There have also been reports of talking dolls, glowing red eyes, and tapping sounds on closed doors.

3. The Grove (Jefferson)

The Grove, also called the Stilley-Young House, is located in Jefferson. The historic home was built in 1861, and has been owned by several families, including the families of W. Frank Stilley and Charlie Young. In the 1990s, the building had a short stint as a successful restaurant, but today The Grove is better known for being the most haunted house in Texas. The home is rumored to be the site of several unmarked graves, and many owners have heard wailing in empty rooms, seen objects moving, and watched ghostly figures glide through the house.

4. (Left) San Fernando Cathedral (San Antonio)

This eighteenth century cathedral is reportedly the oldes church in Texas. Legend says a white stallion gallops in fron of the church at night, and a figure dressed as a monk is knowr to appear in the back of the cathedral. Shadowy figures anc orbs have also been photographed in pictures of the church

5. (Below and Right) Terlingua Ghost Town (Terlingua)

The population of Terlingua is less than 100 today, but in the early 1900s, thousands flocked to the area to mine for cinnabar, the mineral from which mercury is extracted. By 1903, deaths from mercury poisoning and inadequate mining conditions became commonplace, and the victims were buried in the local cemetery. The town was also hit by the flu epidemic of 1918, filling up more graves. Terlingua is one of the only towns in the country where the dead outnumber the living, giving the area a somber, eerie atmosphere.

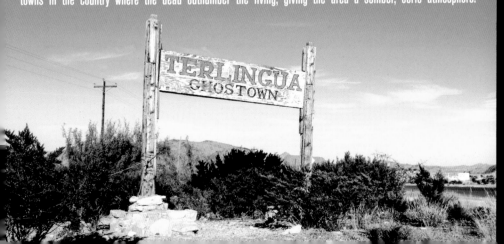

Texas

7. (Above) Driskill Hotel (Austin)

Built in the 1880s, Austin's Driskill Hotel was developed by a cattle baron named Jesse Driskill. The hotel is infamous for deaths that have occurred on its grounds; these deaths include a young girl who died when she fell from a staircase and two brides who died by suicide in the same bathtub exactly 20 years apart. The spirit of Jesse Driskill is also known to haunt the hotel's premises.

6. (Right) Hotel Galvez (Galveston)

This 226-room hotel in Galveston opened in 1911. The U.S. Coast Guard occupied the property during World War II; after a temporary closure in the 1950s, the hotel reopened by the 1960s and ultimately drew plenty of famous guests. It's also haunted by the spirit of a seaman's widow; the widow took her own life after she learned that her husband's ship had sunk

8. (Right) Marfa Lights (Marfa)

Just east of the small town of Marfa, visitors have observed an unusual phenomenon for more than a century. Known as the Marfa Lights, or ghost lights, these orbs of brightness have appeared near U.S. Route 67 since at least 1883, when a cowhand saw a flickering light that had no obvious source. Since then, the lights have been spotted on a regular basis, appearing suddenly over the barren desert, sometimes stationary and sometimes darting around erratically. While scientists have tried to explain them, their origin is still unknown.

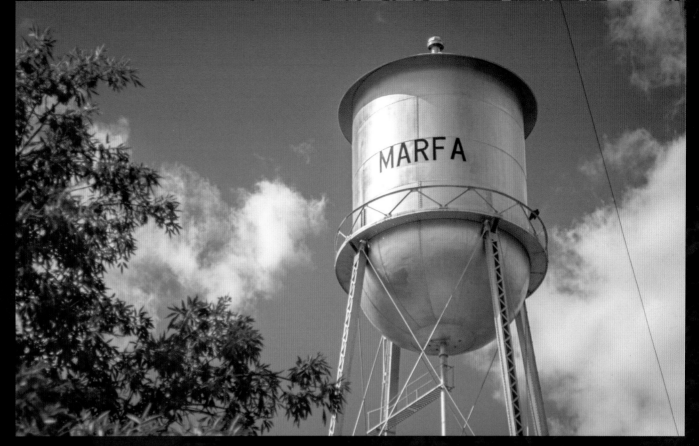

9. (Left) USS *Lexington* (Corpus Christi)

10. Haunted Hill House (Mineral Wells)

Utah

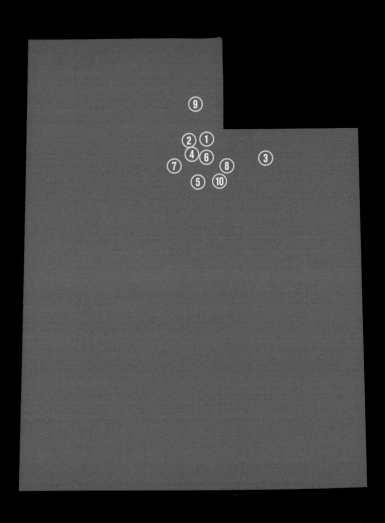

2. (Above and Below) McCune Mansion (Salt Lake City)

Located in the Capitol Hill neighborhood of Salt Lake City, the Alfred McCune Home was named for its owner, a successful railroad builder. Constructed in 1900, the home features materials that were shipped from all over the world, including mahogany wood from South Africa and roof tiles from the Netherlands. With so much attention to detail, it's no wonder that McCune and his family are said to still haunt their beloved mansion. Lights turn on and off, doors lock and unlock, and voices and music are sometimes heard.

1. Mountain Meadows Massacre Site (Mountain Meadows)

In 1857, a wagon train of families known as the Baker-Fancher party was crossing through Utah on their way to California. As they camped at an area known as Mountain Meadows, they were attacked by members of the Utah Territorial Militia, who killed all 120 members of the party, with the exception of 17 children. Historians attribute the massacre to hysteria over a possible invasion of Mormon territory; whatever the cause, visitors to the massacre site insist the victims haunt the area today.

3. (Above) Moon Lake (Duchesne County)

Moon Lake is a picturesque high mountain reservoir in Duchesne County known for its fishing, hiking, and camping. But it's also known for a spooky story that keeps many campers awake all night. According to legend, visitors to the lake have been approached by a young girl with wet hair and clothing, shivering from cold, who asks for help. But if someone approaches the girl, she vanishes. Others hear screams and splashing in the dead of night. Rumor says a girl drowned in the lake years ago, and it is her ghost who now haunts the shore.

4. Rio Grande Depot (Salt Lake City)

A spirit known as the Purple Lady supposedly haunts the Depot. She was killed by a train during a fight with her fiance in the early twentieth century; ghost hunters say she wears a purple hat and dress.

5. Rock Canyon Trail (Provo)

Magnificent during the day, this infamous trail turns incredibly creepy by night. Numerous deaths have occurred on this trail over the decades; hikers report hearing screams and footsteps along the path.

6. Fort Douglas (Salt Lake City)

Multiple murders and suicides occurred here in the late nineteenth and early twentieth centuries. The spirits of the dead, including one ghost who wears a Civil War-era uniform, haunt the garrison today.

7. Old Tooele Hospital (Tooele)

8. Park City Silver Mines (Park City)

9. (Above) The Bigelow Hotel (Ogden)

The Bigelow Hotel in Ogden opened in 1927; it holds the record for the largest hotel in the city. In 1933, the Italian Renaissance Revival-style hotel was renamed the Ben Lomand Hotel, and in 2019, the building was converted to the Bigelow Apartments. But renters may not be alone in their homes, as the Bigelow has a long history of hauntings. Elevators in the building have been known to move on their own and stop on random floors, the scent of old-fashioned perfume lingers in the air, and cold spots are found throughout the building.

10. (Above) Cottonwood Paper Mill (Cottonwood Heights)

The Cottonwood Paper Mill was built in 1883. During its operation, the mill could produce up to five tons of paper per day. But after a fire in 1893, the mill closed down and the building was repurposed as a dance hall. Now abandoned, the site is known for its foreboding ambiance and rumors of ghosts. Some say the shadowy figure of a hanging man appears in the mill at night; others swear the lights turn on and off, despite the building's lack of electricity.

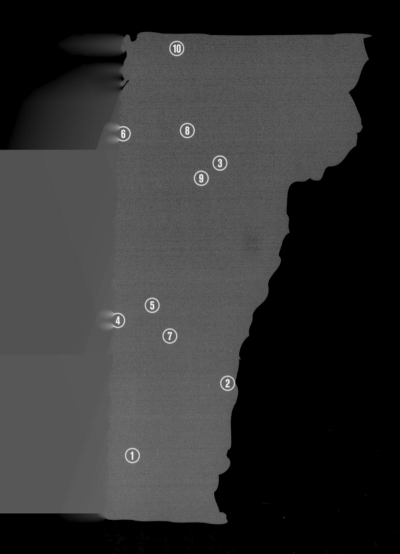

... Mountain (Glastenbury)

...ins in Vermont, Glastenbury Mountain reaches an elevation of 3,748 feet. The spot is ... Long Trail, a hiking trail that runs the length of the state and passes over the summit. But ... altogether, due to its reputation as a site of mysterious disappearances. Between 1945 ... ...nished on the mountain. Only one body was ever found, and no cause of death could be ... ... the mountain is home to a Bigfoot-like creature, while others blame paranormal activity.

...ouse Inn (Springfield)

...nt Cemetery (Montpelier)

4. (Above) Lake Bomoseen (Rutland County)

With a surface area of approximately 2,400 acres, Lake Bomoseen in Rutland County is the largest lake that lies entire... within the state. The lake has been a popular spot for boating, camping, and fishing for decades. But one boat has bee... frightening lake-goers since the early 1900s. Legend says that three quarry workers were rowing a boat across th... lake when they mysteriously disappeared. The trio was never found, but their empty rowboat later washed ashor... Now, visitors to the lake report seeing an empty rowboat on the lake at night; the boat glides silently across the wate...

5. Eddy House (Chittenden)

This creepy house was once the home of Zepaniah Eddy. Eddy's children, William and Horatio, reported... interacted with ghosts and were even expelled from school for levitating books and desks. The children ultimatel... moved back into the house and converted the home into an inn, where they performed séances for eager guest...

6. University of Vermont (Burlington)

An abundance of ghosts haunt Vermont's largest university. One of them is the spirit of John E. Booth, the forme... owner of the school's public relations building. Booth's spirit is known to make banging sounds and even spea...

7. Bowman House (Cuttingsville)

The spirit of a woman named Jennie Bowman supposedly haunts this home's grounds. She was th... wife of John P. Bowman; the couple married in 1849 and were in wedlock until Jennie's death in 188... After her death, John built a mausoleum in honor of his late wife. Following John's death, a wi...

9. (Above) Norwich University (Northfield)

This university is the oldest private military college in the United States; it is described by the U.S. military as the "Birthplace of ROTC." With more than 200 years of history, the school has its fair share of ghost stories, many of which stem from Alumni Hall, the oldest building on campus. Students complain of belongings flying off shelves, banging noises on doors, alarm clocks going off at random times, and shadowy figures in dorm rooms.

8. (Above and Below) Emily's Bridge (Stowe)

The Gold Brook Covered Bridge sits in Stowe; locals know it better as Emily's Bridge. In the 1850s, a poor girl named Emily fell in love with a man from a rich family. The man's family refused to allow their son to marry a poor girl, so the two lovers planned to meet at the bridge to run away. But the man never showed up, leaving Emily distraught. Emily then jumped to her death, and her restless spirit now haunts the bridge.

10. (Above) Enosburg Falls Opera House (Enosburg Falls)

The Enosburg Opera House in Enosburg Falls was built in 1892 and gifted to the town by B.J. Kendall, a wealthy local pharmacist. The building is used for theater performances and as the town's meeting hall, but the house is also popular with ghost hunters, who come to find a ghost named Willy. Rumor says that Willy, the son of a workman in the building, died alone in the attic after breaking his leg. Now, Willy supposedly moves props and scripts, and his footsteps can be heard in the attic.

Virginia

1. (Below) Cold Harbor Battlefield (Mechanicsville)

Between May 31 and June 12, 1864, one of the bloodiest battles of the Civil War took place at the Cold Harbor Battlefield in Mechanicsville. Despite the Union fighting with almost twice as many men, the Confederates won the battle; however, neither side escaped unscathed, and there were more than 17,000 casualties. It's no wonder then that this battlefield is considered to be one of the most haunted military sites in the country. Visitors have felt the boom of artillery fire, smelled gunpowder, and seen heavy, unexplainable fog throughout the grounds.

2. (Above and Right) Bacon's Castle (Surry)

Considered to be the oldest brick dwelling in the United States, Bacon's Castle was built in 1665. Arthur Allen constructed this home, but it came to be known as Bacon's Castle when it was occupied by followers of Nathaniel Bacon during Bacon's Rebellion in 1676. With more than 350 years of history—including secret affairs, untimely deaths, and Native American raids—the house is believed to be one of the most haunted in the state. Visitors have seen fiery orbs, ghostly disembodied heads, and objects moving, as well as heard loud footsteps and voices.

3. (Left) Peyton Randolph House (Williamsburg)

Now a museum in Colonial Williamsburg, the Peyton Randolph House was the home of the first President of the Continental Congress. The house was built in 1715, and it served as a hospital during both the Revolutionary War and the Civil War, which perhaps explains its reputation as a haunted house. Visitors have felt ghostly, icy hands touch their shoulders, seen furniture move on its own, and heard voices. Security guards even recall an incident where a fire extinguisher was emptied in the locked, vacant house.

Virginia

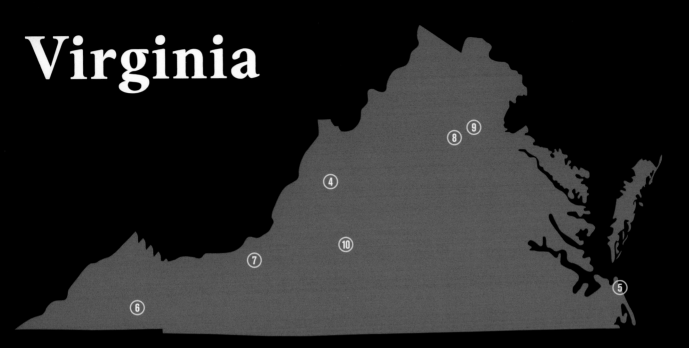

5. Ferry Plantation House (Virginia Beach)

This property dates back hundreds of years to when Native Americans constructed towns along the nearby Lynnhaven River. Multiple courthouses were later built on the site; in the 1830s, the brick house was erected. Today, the 10-room house is home to multiple ghosts, including a young girl, a former slave, and a spirit known as the Lady in White.

4. (Above) Stonewall Jackson Cemetery (Lexington)

This cemetery is the resting spot of Confederate general Stonewall Jackson. Visitors regularly report sightings of Jackson and Robert E. Lee riding on horseback!

6. (Above) Martha Washington Hotel & Spa (Abingdon)

War of 1812 hero and general Francis Preston built this magnificent home in 1832. Since its inception, the home (and later hotel) has hosted some of America's most famous celebrities and leaders, including Jimmy Carter, Harry Truman, Eleanor Roosevelt, and Elizabeth Taylor. It's also the residence of numerous spirits, including a Confederate soldier, former slaves, and even a phantom horse.

7. (Above) St. Albans Sanatorium (Radford)

Radford's infamous sanatorium opened in the early twentieth century, where it was a popular hospital for the mentally ill until the end of the 1990s. Sadly, multiple suicides and other deaths occurred during its operation. Today, the abandoned facility is downright creepy: graffitied, crumbling walls create an unsettling atmosphere. It's of little surprise, then, that the spirits of the complex's former patients still haunt the hospital's grounds.

8. (Right) Exchange Hotel (Gordonsville)

This nineteenth century hotel was a hospital for wounded soldiers in the Civil War. In the 1970s, it was designated as a historic place in the National Register of Historic Places. Likely due to its history as an infirmary, the hotel is extremely haunted; visitors regularly report apparitions, random voices, and items that mysteriously move.

9. Graffiti House (Brandy Station)

10. Historic Avenel (Bedford)

Washington

1. (Below) Northern State Mental Hospital (Sedro-Woolley)

This secluded hospital was built on over 1000 acres; for nearly 60 years, it was home to thousands of patients that underwent barbaric treatments. By 1973, though, the facility was virtually abandoned. Today, the hospital's decaying infrastructure evokes an ominous, supernatural atmosphere.

2. (Left) Point Defiance Park (Tacoma)

This exquisite Tacoma park is where the spirit of a 13-year-old girl roams. The girl, Jennifer Marie Bastian, went missing in 1986 during a bike ride; authorities found her body weeks later off the park's Five Mile Drive. Park patrons regularly encounter the girl's spirit, an apparition infamous for her creepy smile.

3. (Right) Thornewood Castle (Lakewood)

Lakewood's eerie Tudor castle was built in the early twentieth century from pieces of a sixteenth century English Elizabethan manor. The finished result is a bustling 27,000-square-foot estate that includes 54 rooms, a sunken garden, and enchanting fountains. The spirit of Chester Thorne, the castle's original owner, supposedly makes appearances around the castle; the ghost of Thorne's wife, Anna, has also been seen sitting in her former room.

4. The Oxford Saloon (Snohomish)

Snohomish's famous saloon was built in 1900. Initially it was a dry goods store before its incarnation as a saloon. Multiple deaths occurred at the site, including the killing of a policeman named Henry. Henry's spirit supposedly haunts the saloon, as that of a woman named Kathleen.

Washington

5. (Below) Mount Baker Theatre (Bellingham)

Known for cold sports, floating orbs, and mysterious voices, this venue first opene[d] in 1927. The spirit of a young woman named Judy also apparently haunts the theate[r]

CODY RVERS
SEP 27 29

8PM

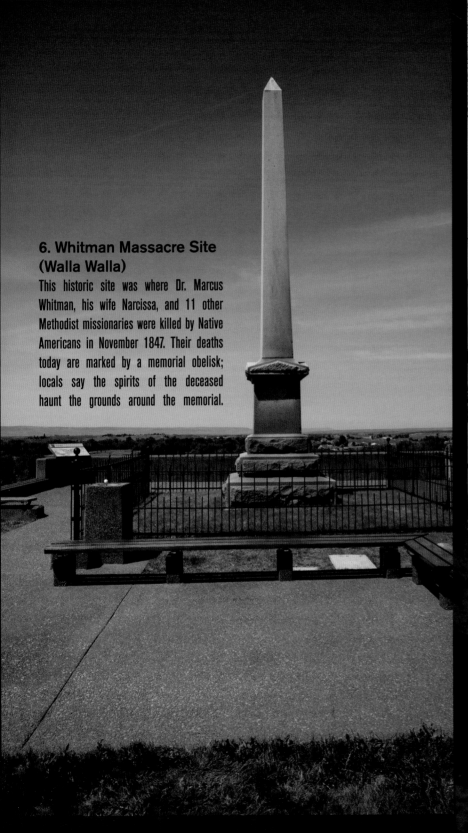

6. Whitman Massacre Site (Walla Walla)

This historic site was where Dr. Marcus Whitman, his wife Narcissa, and 11 other Methodist missionaries were killed by Native Americans in November 1847. Their deaths today are marked by a memorial obelisk; locals say the spirits of the deceased haunt the grounds around the memorial.

7. (Above) Kells Irish Restaurant and Pub (Seattle)

Seattle's creepy pub was built on the grounds of a former funeral home. For decades, all kinds of ominous activity have been reported here; objects regularly shatter, plaster falls from the walls, and ghosts have even been seen passing through the walls. Restaurant staff even say they can smell formaldehyde during work shifts!

8. Rucker Mansion (Everett)

The spirit of a woman known as Mrs. Rucker haunts this historic, 10,000-square-foot home. She supposedly leapt to her death from an upstairs window in the early twentieth century, but her presence remains.

9. Stanwood Hotel and Saloon (Stanwood)

10. Monte Cristo Ghost Town (Snohomish County)

West Virginia

2. (Above) Droop Mountain Battlefield (Hillsboro)

This modern-day state park was the location of one of the Civil War's final battles; the Union army's advance forced the Confederate soldiers to retreat into the northern parts of Virginia. Visitors who roam the park after dark have encountered all kinds of creepy experiences, including a headless ghost, random bright spots, and phantom horses.

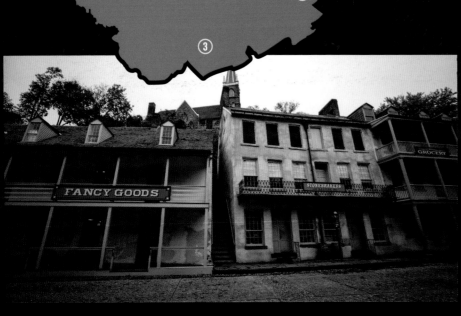

3. (Above) Lake Shawnee Amusement Park (Rock)

This abandoned amusement park has a chilling past. A former Native American burial ground, the site was turned into an amusement park in the 1920s by Conley Snidow. Unfortunately, multiple deaths occurred on the park's grounds over the next several decades; by the mid-1960s, the park was abandoned. In recent years, the site has been a hotspot for paranormal activity, including mysterious cries, screams, and other noises.

1. (Above) Haunted Harpers Ferry (Harpers Ferry)

West Virginia's tourist town is best known for John Brown's raid in 1859. Today, the town is extremely haunted, primarily by Civil War-era spirits (including John Brown himself).

4. (Above) Berkley Castle (Berkeley Springs)

A 15-room mansion, Berkeley Castle was built in the late nineteenth century by a Maryland businessman for his young bride, Rosa Suit. It was later a tourist destination and was ultimately added to the National Register of Historic Places. The castle is haunted by the spirit of Suit. In 2020, ghost hunters purchased the mansion for $360,000.

5. (Above) Point Pleasant Mothman (Point Pleasant)

6. (Above) West Virginia Penitentiary (Moundsville)

Moundsville's Gothic-style prison was built in 1866; it housed inmates for nearly 130 years until its 1995 closure. The structure covers 19 acres and features plenty of 35-square-foot prison cells. Ninety-four men were executed at the prison, but some of those inmates never left.

7. Trans-Allegheny Lunatic Asylum (Weston)

This gothic-style hospital operated for 130 years until its closure in 1994. Many of the institution's patients suffered through unsanitary, crowded conditions during their stays; others, however, never left. Paranormal investigators say all kinds of ghosts haunt the asylum's grounds, including Civil War soldiers, a little girl named Lilly, and a heart attack victim named Jesse.

8. Blennerhassett Hotel (Parkersburg)

Parkersburg's historic hotel was constructed in the end of the nineteenth century. It's apparently haunted by its former owner, William Chancellor. Chancellor has been seen by guests in hotel room mirrors wearing a tuxedo!

9. 22 Mine Road (Holden)

The spirit of Mamie Thurman haunts this West Virginia road. The 31-year-old Thurman was murdered in 1932 near the road; a jury later convicted a handyman in her killing. Cars placed in neutral on a near hill near where her body was found are known to roll uphill; Thurman's spirit is known to push the cars uphill!

10. Lewisburg Historic District (Lewisburg)

Wisconsin

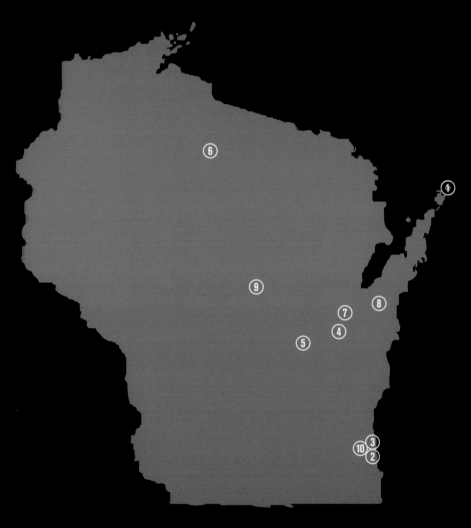

3. (Above and Below) The Pfister Hotel (Milwaukee)
Built in 1893, Milwaukee's Pfister Hotel (formally known as a "Grand Hotel of the West") is the home of numerous ghosts, including that of the spirit of the hotel's founder, Charles Pfister. In addition to Pfister's apparition, guests also regularly report unusual voices, bodiless footsteps, and flickering lights.

1. Nelson's Hall (Washington Island)
Danish immigrant Tom Nelson built this Door County pub in 1899. He invented a powerful (and highly alcoholic) bitters tonic for stomachaches and sea sickness. More than 120 years, his restless spirit is known to hang around his old watering hole; employees frequently encounter footsteps and doors than randomly shut.

2. Brumder Mansion (Milwaukee)
This Milwaukee bed and breakfast is home to all kinds of paranormal occurrences. Guests occasionally see a ghostly woman in a Victorian-era dress walking up and down the mansion's stairs; others have seen unexplained shadows in the mansion's hallways and felt sudden temperature changes during their stays.

4. (Above) Grand Opera House (Oshkosh)

Oshkosh's famous Opera house was built in 1883; it underwent a major renovation in 2009. A former stage manager named Percy Keene apparently haunts the theater's balcony. Some have also seen a phantom dog in the building.

5. Dartford Cemetery (Green Lake)

This rural Wisconsin city is known for its picturesque lake that was considered by Native Americans to be home to a powerful spirit. The city's Dartford Cemetery is known for other kinds of spirits, including Civil War-era soldiers that are known to march around the grounds.

6. Elk Lake Dam (Elk Lake)

The body of a woman named Mary Schlais was found near the dam in 1974. Authorities believe Schlasis was hitchhiking around that time and was picked up by a stranger and killed; her case was never solved. Her spirit has been seen around the dam by fisherman, locals, and visitors.

7. Riverside Cemetery (Appleton)

The ghost of Kate Blood supposedly haunts Appleton's spooky cemetery. Blood died in 1874 at the age of 23; legend says her husband murdered her, while others claim Blood died of tuberculosis. During full moons, blood oozes from the face of her family's tombstone!

8. (Above) Maribel Caves Hotel (Maribel)

A fire in 1985 forced this historic hotel to close; the origins of the blaze were never fully understood. Since its closure, all kinds of paranormal activities have taken place on these grounds, including mysterious lights, footsteps, and voices. A ghost is known to appear in one of the vacant building's windows.

9. Bloody Bride Bridge (Stevens Point)

10. Shaker's Cigar Bar (Milwaukee)

Wyoming

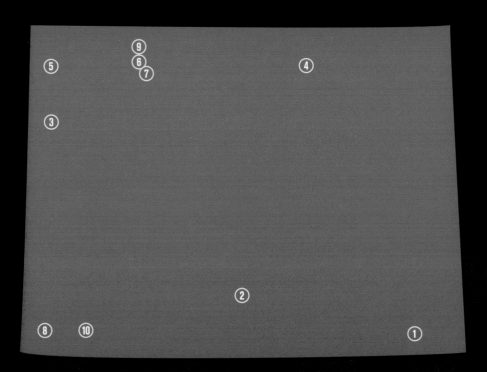

4. (Above and Below) Occidental Hotel (Buffalo)

Buffalo's haunted hotel opened in 1880; it was a popular resting place for travelers on the Bozeman Trail. In its early years the hotel served a handful of famous guests, including Teddy Roosevelt and Buffalo Bill Body. Unfortunately, the Occidental's popularity waned after the Great Depression; the building was heavily remodeled at the end of the century in an attempt to return it to its old glory self. Today, several creepy spirits haunt the hotel, including the ghost of a former prostitute's young daughter.

1. Historic Plains Hotel (Cheyenne)

This extravagant hotel was erected in 1911. It has hosted dignitaries, celebrities, and plenty of honeymooners. One of those honeymooners, a bride named Rosie, never left. During her stay, Rosie spotted her new husband cheating on her with a prostitute; enraged, the bride killed both of them with her husband's gun and then died by suicide. Today, Rosie's spirit can be found roaming the hotel's second floor.

2. Wyoming Frontier Prison (Rawlins)

This infamous prison was known for housing some of Wyoming's most violent criminals. When it opened in the early twentieth century there was no electricity or hot water. By the time of the prison's closure in 1981, it had earned a brutal reputation for its awful conditions. Numerous ghosts still haunt its grounds, most of whom are the spirits of convicts who never left.

3. Wort Hotel (Jackson Hole)

The Wort family built this quaint hotel in 1941. In the 1960s, two children were killed by a family member who was staying in one of the rooms. Today, the ghosts of the children stalk the hotel's halls.

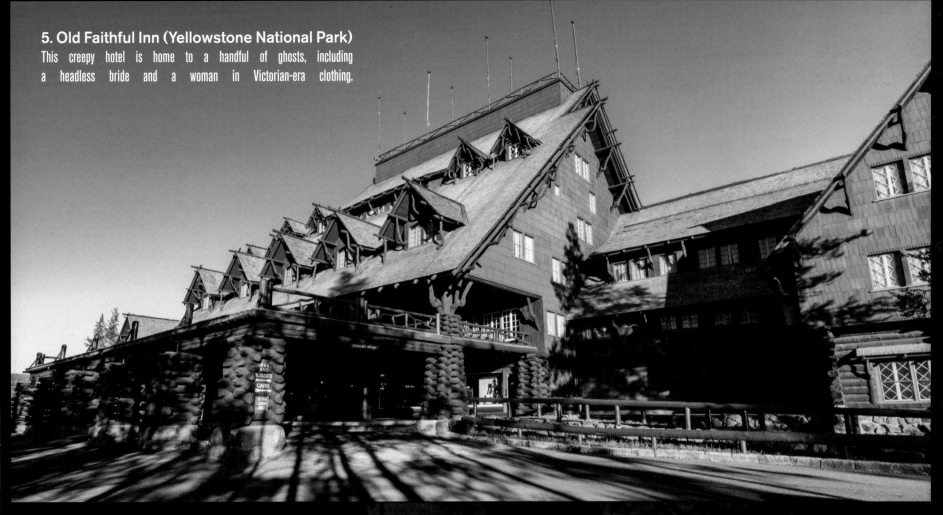

5. Old Faithful Inn (Yellowstone National Park)
This creepy hotel is home to a handful of ghosts, including a headless bride and a woman in Victorian-era clothing.

6. (Left) Irma Hotel (Cody)
Buffalo Bill Cody built the Irma Hotel in 1902. Several ghosts haunt its premises today; the spirits are known for their harmless pranks, such as shuffling the luggage of guests.

Wyoming

7. (Right) Cedar Mountain (Cody)

This northern Wyoming mountain was once called "Spirit Mountain" by Native American tribes. Though the mountain is popular with hikers, it's also haunted. Hikers regularly hear disembodied footsteps along hiking trails; locals believe the ghost of Buffalo Bill Cody walks the mountain

8. (Left) Fort Bridger State Historic Site (Fort Bridger)

The spirit of a dog named Thornburgh reportedly haunts this historic site. He once saved a young child's life; today, he guards the site's burial grounds.

9. Heart Mountain Relocation Center (Park County)

10. Sweetwater County Library (Green River)